CAMBRIDGE LIBRARY COLLECTION

Books of enduring scholarly value

Religion

For centuries, scripture and theology were the focus of prodigious amounts
of scholarship and publishing, dominated in the English-speaking world
by the work of Protestant Christians. Enlightenment philosophy and
science, anthropology, ethnology and the colonial experience all brought
new perspectives, lively debates and heated controversies to the study of
religion and its role in the world, many of which continue to this day. This
series explores the editing and interpretation of religious texts, the history of
religious ideas and institutions, and not least the encounter between religion
and science.

Cambridge and Other Sermons

First published in 1898, this collection of sermons by the Irish-born
Cambridge biblical scholar and theologian Fenton John Anthony Hort
distils over thirty years' work as a pastor. Compiled by the author's son six
years after Hort's death, this book contains twenty-four sermons, organised
to correspond with the Church calendar. Written for school children,
Cambridge college chapels, and the congregation of Hort's own parish in
Hertfordshire, many of the sermons in this collection were delivered on
more than one occasion and have consequently been revised many times. As
Hort's son points out, they appear here in their 'ultimate form', perfected over
three decades. First preached over a century ago, Hort's lucid prose makes his
work easily accessible. Written in deceptively simple language, the care and
precision found in Hort's better-known academic work are also evident in his
sermons, which are articulated with grace and clarity.

Cambridge University Press has long been a pioneer in the reissuing of out-of-print titles from its own backlist, producing digital reprints of books that are still sought after by scholars and students but could not be reprinted economically using traditional technology. The Cambridge Library Collection extends this activity to a wider range of books which are still of importance to researchers and professionals, either for the source material they contain, or as landmarks in the history of their academic discipline.

Drawing from the world-renowned collections in the Cambridge University Library, and guided by the advice of experts in each subject area, Cambridge University Press is using state-of-the-art scanning machines in its own Printing House to capture the content of each book selected for inclusion. The files are processed to give a consistently clear, crisp image, and the books finished to the high quality standard for which the Press is recognised around the world. The latest print-on-demand technology ensures that the books will remain available indefinitely, and that orders for single or multiple copies can quickly be supplied.

The Cambridge Library Collection will bring back to life books of enduring scholarly value (including out-of-copyright works originally issued by other publishers) across a wide range of disciplines in the humanities and social sciences and in science and technology.

Cambridge and Other Sermons

FENTON JOHN ANTHONY HORT

CAMBRIDGE UNIVERSITY PRESS

Cambridge, New York, Melbourne, Madrid, Cape Town, Singapore,
São Paolo, Delhi, Dubai, Tokyo

Published in the United States of America by Cambridge University Press, New York

www.cambridge.org
Information on this title: www.cambridge.org/9781108007566

© in this compilation Cambridge University Press 2009

This edition first published 1898
This digitally printed version 2009

ISBN 978-1-108-00756-6 Paperback

CAMBRIDGE AND OTHER SERMONS

CAMBRIDGE & OTHER SERMONS

BY

FENTON JOHN ANTHONY HORT

D.D., D.C.L., LL.D.

SOMETIME HULSEAN PROFESSOR
AND LADY MARGARET'S READER IN DIVINITY IN THE
UNIVERSITY OF CAMBRIDGE

London

MACMILLAN AND CO., Limited

NEW YORK: THE MACMILLAN COMPANY

1898

GLASGOW: PRINTED AT THE UNIVERSITY PRESS
BY ROBERT MACLEHOSE AND CO.

PREFATORY NOTE

THESE twenty-four sermons are arranged in a series corresponding to the Church's year ; they are not however of one uniform character. Most of them were preached more than once, generally with considerable alteration and adaptation : nearly all are here printed in their ultimate form. Though all are alike in simplicity of language, those written for a village congregation naturally present more elementary aspects of faith and service than those intended for a college chapel or the University church. Since they range over a period of over thirty years, it might be said that those of earlier date do not perhaps represent the author's maturest thought ; but the frequent revision which most of them underwent makes it probable that little, if anything, is here printed which he would have disowned. It is hoped that some of the many who found in Dr. Hort's *Village Sermons* strength and instruction may also welcome these more various discourses from the same mind : in all essentials the characteristics of both series are the same.

The texts and other quotations from the Bible are printed as they stand in the manuscript : it will be noticed that it was often the preacher's practice to give an independent rendering identical with neither English version. In two cases (Nos. XI. and XXII.) I have ventured to supply a title. Nos. VII. and VIII., as also XIX. and XX., were preached consecutively.

A. F. HORT.

CONTENTS

I.

VII.

XIV.

XV.

XVI.

XVII.

XVIII.

XIX.

XX.

CAMBRIDGE AND OTHER SERMONS

I

THE PROBATION OF THE JEWS BY THE LIGHT

Emmanuel College Chapel, First Sunday in Advent, 1877.

"THEN Jesus said unto them, Yet a little while is the light with
you. Walk while ye have the light, lest darkness come upon you :
for he that walketh in darkness knoweth not whither he goeth. While
ye have light, believe in the light, that ye may be the children of light.
These things spake Jesus, and departed, and did hide himself from
them."—*John* xii. 35 f.

THE Advent messages of to-day, which speak to us
from Collect, Epistle, and Gospel, and from the prophetic lessons of Isaiah, find a meeting-point and
explanation in the strangely impressive record from
St. John's Gospel which chances to be our second
lesson for this afternoon. No one surely can listen
to the march of those measured verses without feeling their tremendous power. But the impression
becomes at once deepened and diversified, if we set
ourselves to spell out a little of their meaning; and
especially if, as a first step, we observe where they
stand in the order of the Gospel. The next chapter,
the thirteenth, begins the second part of St. John's

A

narrative, the record of the words and deeds accompanying our Lord's departure out of the world that He might return to the Father, belonging therefore partly to the last evening, night, and day of His earthly life, partly to His manifestations of Himself to the unsealed eyes of disciples after His resurrection. The record of His ministry, in the strict sense of the word, thus ends with the twelfth chapter, and our lesson of to-day closes the story with a single significant scene, and the words which were needed to bring out its force.

For some time back the signs of the approaching crisis had been thickening. The unbelief of the Jews, who refused to recognize their own King, had turned from suspicion to hatred. The raising of Lazarus had quickened hatred with alarm, and brought about a definite purpose of murder. Any lurking hesitation was removed, when the shouts of the multitude were heard welcoming the entry of Jesus of Nazareth into the city, and the blinded Pharisees cried, "Behold, the world is gone away after him." Then St. John passes to the last event of the ministry, which it is needful for his purpose to tell. Among the crowds who had come up, like Jesus Himself, to worship at the national festival, were certain Greeks, men who had adopted the Jewish faith and law, but were of alien race and traditions. These Greeks found their way to Philip and expressed a desire to see Jesus. Philip spoke of the request to his townsman and brother apostle, Andrew, and they together came and made it known to the Lord. The Lord's answer showed at once that He recognized this unobtrusive incident of quiet progress and encouragement as the definitive sign that the end was now indeed nigh at hand. His own personal ministry, as fixed in God's counsel, was to be a ministry to Jews. The Jews as a body had been rejecting it, and now Gentiles were seeking to receive it, and thereby marking that the Jewish rejection was no longer tendency only, but well-nigh a deliberate decision. Two opposing visions therefore rose up before His soul at once: the woeful doom of Israel, the glorious reception of the gospel by the nations of the world. And these two visions of mankind were reflected in two corresponding visions of Himself and His appointed destiny. His rejection by Israel must be consummated by His death at the hands of Israel, and that death of His would be the source of His world-wide triumph, the beginning of a new ministry, which should go on multiplying from age to age.

"The hour is come," He said, "that the Son of man should be glorified." Then He went on to declare the law of glorification which prevails wherever God is King. It is only by falling into the ground and dying that the corn of wheat can bear much fruit. A true Son of Man must regard his soul or earthly life as that seed corn. He must be willing to cast it into the ground when God commands, knowing that God will raise it into a life eternal. No true servant or disciple has a right to shrink from this destiny. "If any man," He said, "serve Me, let him follow Me." Yet this clear faith did not render the soul of that perfect Son of Man inaccessible to the troublings of ordinary human fears. "Now is my soul troubled, and what shall I say? Father, save me from this hour." Yet as soon as the conflict came, the will sided with the faith. In a moment the second word was spoken. "But for this cause came I into this hour." And so the prayer of trouble rose up into the prayer of victorious faith, "Father, glorify thy name." By Him no outward sign that the prayer had been heard was needed: for Him the inward witness sufficed. But to the true yet imperfect faith of disciples a reassuring voice out of heaven was vouchsafed, a voice to them, an inarticulate thunder to others. The momentary strife in His soul was over, and all that was personal henceforth sunk in the thought of the powers contending for possession of the human race, and the deliverance of the captives which His death should accomplish. "Now is there a judgment of this world, now shall the ruler of this world be cast out: and I, if I be lifted up out of the earth, will draw all men unto myself." The world was about to judge Him, and in so doing would judge itself. The usurping ruler of this world, the inspirer of its cruel and jealous intents, was about to cast Him out, and in so doing would cast himself out: while He, the true King, thus cast out of the earth by the world and its ruler, would thereby be lifted up out of the earth by an exaltation of which His uplifting on the Cross would be a visible sign, and by that uplifting He should draw all men upwards to His own high estate.

The multitude had desired a Christ after their

own magnified likeness, a softened and corrected
Herod, and such they had expected the Nazarene
whom they had escorted over the Mount of Olives
to show Himself. To men filled with these expectations His present language about a Son of Man was
very baffling. They could not in their thoughts
bring the Christ and the Son of Man together.
They began to feel that they had made a mistake in
their choice. " Who," they asked, " who is this Son
of man ? " Then came the words of the text, words
prophetic of doom, yet not pronouncing doom; words
rather of tender expostulation, implying that there
was yet a pause within which all things were possible before the decisive hour should strike, though
even now it was about to strike ; words swelling at
the last to a note of bright and cheerful encouragement: " Yet a little while the light is in you. Walk.
while ye have the light, lest darkness overtake you:
and he that walketh in the darkness knoweth not
whither he goeth. While ye have the light, believe
on the light, that ye may become sons of light."

Such were the possibilities of that moment. We
all know how sadly they failed to become facts.
St. John, who had seen the whole tragedy unroll
itself, and whose heart had been torn by the crimes
and by the miseries of his own people, concludes
his narrative with a single sentence expressing the
external ending of that scene, expressing also the
inward fact of spiritual history, of which the cata-
strophe of that tragedy was the necessary fruit:
" These things spake Jesus, and departed, and was
hidden from them." He went His way; they theirs.

For a while the light had been among them, and they had found some pleasure in its radiance and warmth. But when it came to search out the dark places of their hearts and make serious claims on their allegiance, they decided that they could wel-- come it no more ; and so it dwelt no longer among them, but became hidden from their sight.

To these few words of history St. John appends some thoughts of his own, first on the unbelief of the Jews, and then on a divine purpose behind their unbelief—both foreshadowed in the great prophetic book of glad tidings. He thus at once sounds the lowest depths of the curse that had fallen on Israel, and teaches us not to forget that all these things belong to the encompassing mystery of Providence, and can only be understood in the light of the mind and character of Him whose will *is* Providence. If we desire more explicit language, we shall find it in those chapters of the Epistle to the Romans in which St. Paul faces boldly this same fatal unbelief of Israel, and its seeming contradiction to the pro- mises of God; quotes freely some of the same and other like startling words of the Old Testament; and then lays it down broadly, as the result of his whole survey, that God hath concluded them all under unbelief that He might have mercy upon all.

Nothing of this is said by St. John, though it is difficult to believe that the remembrance of words spoken by Christ Himself (such, for instance, as those about the results of His lifting up out of the earth) was not presenting to his mind a similar vision when he pointed thus fearlessly to the original

counsel of God. But in the closing paragraph of
this chapter and lesson he takes care in another way
that his record of the ministry of the Saviour shall
not end with the burden of condemnation, by sub-
joining yet more words of our Lord which carry on
in a calmer strain the teaching of the former verses.
Here too there is mention of light and darkness, of
belief and rejection, and therefore also of judgment.
But there is also clear statement of the purpose of
Christ's coming into the world: " I am come a light
into the world, that whosoever believeth in me
should not abide in the darkness." " I came not
that I might judge the world, but that I might save
the world." And along with these declarations
about His own work, Christ at the beginning and
the end declares Himself once more, as He had
often done before, to be the true image of the
Father: " He that believeth on me, believeth not on
me but on him that sent me; and he that beholdeth
me, beholdeth him that sent me." " What things I
speak, as the Father hath said unto me so I speak."
And thus the last message of His ministry is its
perfect conformity with the Supreme Will, and the
certainty with which we may conclude from the prevailing character of His ministry to the prevailing
character of the Will that is over all. Men had
to do not with a sovereign enforcing his behests,
but with a Father, the source of life bestowing life
on the only conditions on which reasonable and free
creatures could receive it. The perfectly obedient
Son could say, " I know that his commandment is
eternal life."

The review of the contents of this lesson (brief though it be, considering the range of subjects included in the lesson) has left but little time for drawing out the special force of its Advent teaching. Yet it is equally true that Advent thoughts have been accompanying us all along. The whole lesson is the story of a great probation and its close. To some the mention of a probation is in itself an offence. A holy and wise theologian of recent times was accustomed to set up the idea of divine education against that of divine probation. It is perhaps well that some should be found to take up this extreme position, since so much harm has been done to theology by setting forth probation as a complete account of God's moral dealings with man. But I cannot see that there is any contradiction between the two ideas; and unless we acknowledge probation as part of God's education of His children, it seems to me that we throw away a large part of human experience, as well as do violence to much clear teaching of Scripture. Although there is a continuity in all our lives, they are also broken into various stages with different opportunities and responsibilities, and few indeed can bring home to themselves the solemn charge with which they are entrusted from hour to hour, who do not recognize themselves as called to account from time to time by God above for the faithfulness with which they have executed their stewardship. The duties which He lays upon them are appointed for their own benefit as well as the benefit of His other creatures; but they cannot live the true human life if they emulate the unconscious growth of beings without wills, and count it an unworthy thing to fulfil commandments, though they be the commandments of the life-giving God.

If the lesson of to-day reminds us of the most memorable instance of a probation, and of the condemnation pronounced on unprofitable servants, it likewise brings vividly before us the often forgotten truth that divine judgment, whatever else it may be, is a light, and invested with all the beneficent properties of light. Our common ways are at best but ways of twilight, of light and darkness mingled. When Christ comes among men, when His words and acts are felt as a forceful presence, there arises a dividing between the light and the darkness, and this is judgment. God's judgments without are the necessary proclamations of His discerning and judging mind, made necessary by our neglect to judge ourselves within. We are loth to believe that our twilight is not all light, or what will do as well; and so we walk on still in darkness, or what is much the same as darkness. Our lives of confused and indolent acquiescence are exactly described in our Lord's words about him who " knoweth not whither he goeth." In this condition we have no definite and sedulously followed purpose. Nay, even from hour to hour we are the victims of endless delusion. In our twilight we think we see many things; but we see nothing as it really is.

Let us then welcome the call to judgment, in whatever accent it comes, for it means a call to choose and follow the light. Let us welcome the call to choose and follow the light, for it means a call to recognize and follow Him who gave Himself for us. The Light of lights for us is not a diffused luminousness, but a living Saviour on whom we can set our hearts in loving trust. Such a Light, so believed in, will mould us by degrees into its own likeness, making us not only obedient servants of Light, but sons of Light, ever drawing truth and goodness together from the Father of lights in whom they are essentially one, ever transmitting to our fellowmen whatever truth and goodness we may have been enabled to receive from that heavenly fountain.

II

THE REVELATION TO THE SHEPHERDS

Great Saint Mary's Church, before the University.   Christmas Day, 1883.

"AND the angel said unto them, Be not afraid, for behold I bring you good tidings of great joy which shall be to all the people: for there is born to you this day in the city of David a Saviour, which is Christ the Lord.   And this is the sign unto you : ye shall find a babe wrapped in swaddling clothes, and lying in a manger."—*Luke* ii. 10-12 (R.V.).

THE birth of our Lord, like His resurrection, is inseparably bound up for the mind of Christendom with the manifestations which followed it. It is for the most part in the presence of the shepherds of Judah and the Magian pilgrims from the East that the Holy Babe presents Himself to our inward eye. For many of us, in this even more than in other parts of Biblical history, our impressions have been unconsciously formed by pictures. The shepherds on the one side, the three kings from the East on the other, united in adoration of the newly-born Child in the midst, are constant elements of a variously represented scene, familiar to us through the devotion or the skill of several generations of painters. The conception which we have derived from this imaginative combination of incidents historically distinct is essentially a true one. Each of the two evangelists who record the Nativity associates it in the closest manner with one of these two manifestations; and again it is only when the two events are brought together that their full significance becomes apparent. The two narratives are in all their particulars transparently independent of each other, and written without reference to each other; and yet in an unexpected way they are complementary to each other in their prophetic import. Together they shadow forth the union of the two peoples, Jew and Gentile, in the one new faith, in fulfilment of the highest aspirations of the elder prophets. But it is the evangelist of the Gentile Church that records the revelation of the Nativity to men of the faithful remnant of God's ancient people, and their homage of praise and thanksgiving: while it is the evangelist of the Hebrew Church that records the discovery of the Nativity by patient and devout watchers from among the heathen world, and their characteristic homage of costly gifts.

In the light of this two-fold manifestation of the Nativity we can read more clearly the force of the several words spoken by the angel to the shepherds, though indeed by themselves they are not difficult to interpret, if we take them in their literal simplicity. The first words, " Fear not," merely prepare the way for what was to follow. In the stillness of the night-watch, patiently waiting, and yet in so doing

pursuing their appointed task, the shepherds had
been brought suddenly face to face with the hidden
world above. " An angel of Jehovah" stood before
them in visible presence. "A glory of Jehovah
shone round about them," a blaze of light indicating
in outward symbol the realm out of which the
angel had descended, and the ineffable glory about
Jehovah's throne. At these sights the shepherds
" feared with a great fear." Such fear was the first
step towards a due reception of the message to
come. But it was not intended to remain in this its
first state of mere fear for more than a few moments.
At the command, " Fear not," it was to rise into
a fervent awe, sustaining a heavenly gladness. The
messenger and the vision were not come upon them
as heralds of doom, or any terrible form of visitation.
" Fear not, for behold I bring you good tidings of a
great joy which shall be to all the people."

" I bring you good tidings." Here at the outset
the messenger describes his office by the word which
the Isaiah of the exile had several times employed
for Jehovah's mission of comfort to His suffering
people, and which must thenceforward have been
associated with every hope of divine renewal and
restoration. But he passes on at once to the subject
of the message. It is "a great joy which shall be to
all the people." Now that the disturbing fear which
had at first seized on the shepherds had been calmed
away, there was no further reference to anything
that was of merely personal concern to themselves.
It is assumed that the joy whereof they will thankfully receive good tidings at the lips of an angel

is a joy which concerns the whole people. Their thoughts were not wholly absorbed in the flocks which they tended, or even in the homes which they had left behind. Their best heritage was to be sons of Israel. The welfare and the hope of Israel must be the theme of the good tidings to which their hearts would most surely respond.

Then follows the announcement of the cause for " a great joy "—" for there is born to you this day a Saviour." The combination of words at once suggests that we have here a yet more distinct echo of another prophecy that no true son of Israel could ever forget. " Thou hast multiplied the nation, thou hast made great to it the joy. They joy before thee as is the joy in harvest, as men exult when they divide the spoil." For a moment Isaiah had turned aside to the mere results of the deliverance which is the occasion of the great joy; to the breaking of the yoke, and staff, and taskmaster's rod; to the destruction of the enemy's warlike equipment as fuel for the fire. But he had quickly returned to the deeper and surer ground for great joy in the divine gift of one who was at once a true child of the household of Israel, and a king destined to reign under a name and with a purpose like Jehovah's own. " For unto us a child is born, unto us a son is given." Thus the recollection of the great joy which had been granted to the people in the dark days of Ahaz would prepare the way for a true perception of the great joy appointed for the people in the days of Herod.

After this echo of Isaiah's words the angel's

message passes on to an explicit description of the character and office of Him who was born that day: He was "a Saviour," a Saviour who was also "an anointed Lord," and that "in David's city." The ruling title "Saviour" must, of course, be understood in such a sense or senses as it could bear to the shepherds. It was no new title for men raised up by God or for God Himself. It would suggest pre-eminently a deliverer from enemies, and so from all things which make war on the life and peace of man. The earlier and cruder ideal of salvation or deliverance, which took no heed of any enemies or evils that did not come from without, was rife enough in these late days. It was the spell by which one false Messiah after another drew to his standard an unrepentant and turbulent multitude. But the prophets had from first to last been unwearied in setting forth the insufficiency of this ideal, which indeed made the Saviour of Israel to differ in no essential respect from the saviour deities of heathen nations; and no one who had entered into the teaching of the prophets could have failed to learn a better faith. Every holy and humble man of heart in Israel by this time knew the futility of deliverance without when unaccompanied by deliverance within. To such men there would have been small satisfaction in release from vassalage to the Roman yoke or from the intestine violence which filled the land, so long as the whole head of the nation was sick, and its whole heart faint. The promises on which they rather rested were such as those in which Jehovah declared that He would "turn his hand upon" the people, and "purely purge away its dross"; "re-deeming Zion through judgment, and her returning ones through righteousness." In a word, their highest hope of a Saviour would be precisely expressed by the language which, as we read in St. Matthew, the angel used in announcing to Joseph the approaching birth: "He shall save his people from their sins." How much indeed was involved in salvation from sin; by what means it could be wrought out; and above all, how the self-mastery and self-surrender which it demanded from the delivered people, were themselves possible only in and through a Saviour above them; these were points that as yet lay in obscurity. For men who knew wherein consisted the fundamental plagues of their nation and of themselves the simple title "Saviour" was a sufficient assurance.

But of the newly-born Saviour Himself there were other characteristics to be named. "A Saviour, who is an anointed Lord." We can hardly doubt that to the ears of men of that generation the compound phrase would suggest the Messiah, the Anointed of Jehovah, whose image had come to unite many scattered lineaments of ancient prophecy. It might represent not unfitly the mysterious desig-nation in the book of Daniel, familiar to us in the form, 'Messiah the Prince'; and, precisely as here, it stands more than once among the Messianic aspira-tions of those pathetic Jewish hymns which, after ages strangely called Psalms of Solomon, written perhaps hardly more than a generation before the time when the Anointed Lord was actually born.

But though the words used by the angel may thus have been charged with Messianic associations, they were doubtless intended to be understood first in their own proper and separate sense. The Saviour who had now come was not merely one of the people whom He was come to save; nor again had He only a secondary or intermediate office in relation to the people, prophetic, priestly, or any other. His office among them was the supreme one, He was a Ruler, a Lord. The Child born to them, the Son given to them, was One ' on whose shoulder the government ' rested.

It was needful however that the nature and origin of the lordship should be distinctly proclaimed. That the Saviour should possess and exercise power was not enough. He was not only a Lord but an Anointed Lord; even as the high priest, in accusing Him to Pilate, described Him as " saying that he himself was an anointed King." In other words, from God came His authority, and from God came the endowments for the exercise of His government. Such was manifestly the signification of the anointing of a king in the Old Testament, and especially in the Psalms. The anointed of Jehovah reigned in Jehovah's name: his title was bound up with the obligation to represent visibly to the people in his own acts the righteous rule of the invisible King above. But the divine consecration was also a fountain of divine power. Jehovah did not leave His representative without the fitting gifts of grace for the arduous tasks of his office. And even so did the Apostles themselves understand

B

the anointing which they recognized as implied in the name Christ, borne by Him to whom it pre-eminently belonged. "Thy holy servant Jesus whom thou didst anoint," such is the language of the lofty prayer with which they greeted the release of St. Peter and St. John, contrasting Him thus with the other lords, the kings of the earth and the rulers, who had been gathered together against Him in Jerusalem. "God anointed him," St. Peter said, on the day on which he learned that the Gentiles had indeed a part in the Gospel, speaking of the good tidings of peace sent through Jesus Christ to the sons of Israel—"God anointed him with the Holy Spirit and with power."

One more characteristic of the Saviour remained. He was not only "an anointed Lord," but "an anointed Lord in David's city." So run the words as read in the sense which their order naturally suggests, and which also carries with it the fittest and most pregnant force. That Bethlehem was the place where He who had been born that day was then to be found is indeed directly implied; and hardly less directly that it was the place of His birth. But this was only a subordinate point in the angel's message. As an external coincidence of event, divinely ordained though it was, it was no more than a sign and symbol of a great and far-reaching truth. The words of Micah, in which the scribes of Jerusalem whom Herod questioned were accustomed to read only a barren geographical prediction, were in the strictest sense a divine pro-phecy, linking together the various ages of Israel's history, and finding a worthy fulfilment not in our Lord's birth only, but in His whole office as the anointed King.

The meaning of this part of the angel's message is indicated in the name by which he designates Bethlehem, which outside this chapter is never called the city of David. Partly in preparation for his record of these words, partly in explanation of the reason why it befel that Joseph and Mary were at Bethlehem when the time came for Mary to be delivered, St. Luke, a few verses earlier, gives Bethlehem this name. But in the Old Testament it belongs exclusively to Jerusalem, or a part of Jerusalem; and we can hardly doubt that, on the lips of most Jews, it must still have meant the city where David had fixed his throne. Yet the language spoken to the shepherds cannot have been altogether new. The watchful care which guarded the memory or the records of ancestral lines of descent might well keep alive, in local usage, an exceptional expression of the local glory associated from of old with a great name. Age after age the shepherd folk of Bethlehem might well be proud to claim for their village the name, ' city of David,' as belonging to it by a worthier title than to the vainglorious and sinful capital. Had not David, and David's ancestors, been, like themselves, shepherds of Bethlehem? Were they not entitled to believe that it was by the pastoral habitudes of Bethlehem that David's childhood and youth had been fashioned, and more than a foundation laid for that experience and discipline by which God had schooled and fitted him for kingship? And now, when the old Jebusite capital had become the capital of a cruel son of Edom reigning by favour of the Roman emperor, as king of the Jews, were they not more than ever justified in regarding Bethlehem as the one true home of David?

The shepherds however were not to be the only recipients of the angel's message. If he spoke in such language as their own circumstances would specially enable them to understand, yet it was also the language which was true for all the people. The David whom prophets and psalmists seem most to have in mind in their visions of a future king is David the shepherd, the David of Bethlehem. Grievously as his own actual government was defaced by shortcomings and crimes which could not be forgotten, he was felt in after-times to be, however imperfectly, an embodiment of a new ideal of kingship, the watchful and tender and sympathetic guardianship of human flocks. Accordingly, when the woes of the people are sorest and the kings least kingly, the prophetic eye turns instinctively to the stock from which David was sprung, the home and neighbourhood which had given him nurture, the employment by which he had been schooled, and finds in them the abiding ground whence a new David, a true and yet a better David's son, shall arise. Isaiah looks for a fresh offshoot to come forth from the stock and roots of Jesse. Micah looks for one to be a ruler in Israel who shall come forth out of Bethlehem Ephratah, little among the thousands of Judah. Thus the title, "An anointed

Lord in David's city," as applied to the babe who
was then lying in Bethlehem, set forth in clear
symbol that He, the Saviour of the people, was not
only a Lord and King, not only a Lord and King
divinely commissioned and divinely endowed, but
also such a Lord and King as the long experience of
history and the manifold teaching of prophets had
marked out the future David to be.

The lofty announcement by the angel was followed by the bare instruction as to the sign by
which the shepherds might recognize the Saviour
Lord of whom they had been hearing. " Ye shall
find a babe wrapped in swaddling clothes, and lying
in a manger."   The sign was doubtless more than a
means of recognition.   It was at the same time a
trial of faith, and also an additional teaching on the
subject of the former announcement.   It was one
thing to hear from an angel's lips that a birth of the
highest moment had taken place that day, another
to look with their own eyes on the helpless babe
Himself, and mark the place in which He lay, and
yet believe firmly that they had been listening to
true words.   They had to face a seeming contradiction of the proclaimed lordship.   The swaddling
clothes seemed to mark the extremity of weakness in
His own person, the negation of all the action of a
free being.   The manger seemed to mark the extremity of lowness in His outward estate: already
the Son of Man had not where to lay His head.

The angel ceased to speak to the shepherds.
There came a pause, during which they were permitted to be listeners to wondrous words not

addressed to themselves, a song of joy and praise
from the heavenly spectators of the new scene just
opening in the mysterious drama of human history.
When its last sounds had died away, and the glory
had faded from the heaven, and only the stars
looked down upon them from above, the shepherds
resolved to go without delay and see that whereof
they had heard. They found what they sought.
They made known to others "concerning the saying
which had been spoken to them." And lastly we
read that "the shepherds returned glorifying and
praising God for all the things that they had heard
and seen, even as it was spoken unto them."

They had been to Bethlehem. They returned to
their flocks and their night-watches in the open
country, and all things went on as they had done
before. The miseries of that distracted time ran
their course unchanged. No outward hardship was
lightened by the birth of the Saviour Lord. Some
score of years must pass before He could show
Himself in any sense an active helper of His people.
The shepherds at Bethlehem were far removed from
His childhood and early manhood at Nazareth. We
cannot tell whether any of them lived to hear and
see Him when He came forth to His ministry. So
far as appears, the message of the angel, the song of
the heavenly host, and the sight of the babe were all
that they gained for their whole lives. Yet this was
more than enough. They glorified and praised God,
for indeed a great joy had arisen for all the people,
though nearly all the people knew it not. They had
waited long for the King to be born; they could

wait long still for Him to be manifested; nay, having
now received a pledge that the hope of Israel was no
delusion, they could go on as before and, if it should
so be, die at their appointed time without having
seen on earth any fresh sign of the salvation that
had entered into the world.

At length the thirty years were passed, and the
manifestation to Israel began; and then it soon was
ended, still visible only to those who had eyes to see,
even in those crowning events through which the
Saviour was glorified.   Out of the little band of
faithful Israelites who knew and owned their Lord
and King an universal Church has grown, and
through the Church a Christendom.   Yet still in our
dulness of heart we are always lapsing into forgetfulness that One who is both Saviour and anointed
Lord is indeed in the midst of us, at all times the
Author, the Pattern, and the Sustainer of all true
and beneficent order in human society.   If we give
heed to His presence, we are too apt either to think
of Him as a Saviour who exercises no rule and
demands no obedience; in other words, a Saviour
ineffectual to save from sin ; or else in our thoughts
to strip His sovereignty of its graciousness, and bring
back in His name a law without a gospel.   The
angel's message, interpreting the whole teaching of
Christmas, meets all these diseases of the spirit.
There is a true analogy between, on the one side,
what the shepherds saw and heard that night in
relation to the revelation through the Ministry, the
Passion, the Resurrection, and the Ascension; and,
on the other hand, the whole Incarnation in relation

to the future unveiling of our Lord Jesus Christ.   In
each case a period of partial darkness stands between
an earlier and a later outburst of light.   But in each
case the light already given has been enough for the
way to be trodden, and we know that the times and
seasons are now as always in God's hand.   The
gospel proper, the gospel to the Apostles, will shine
for us with fresher and more living power if we
approach it through the prelusive and elementary
gospel to the shepherds.   The Apostles themselves
will teach us how in their hands, in accordance with
the Father's eternal purpose, the great joy for all the
people became a great joy for all mankind.

III

THE KING EXPECTED AND FOUND

Great Saint Mary's Church, before the University. Christmas Day, 1879.

"WHERE is he that is born King of the Jews?"—*Matt.* ii. 2.

IN these words is contained that meeting together of Advent and Christmas, in which we learn the truest meaning of each. The spirit of Advent is the spirit of expectation: it looks not back over the past, or down into the present, but forward and upward into the future. Yet its expectation is not of a dim point in the far distance: it is of a coming King and Lord, One who came once in the sight of men in great humility; who, risen above our sight, is with us now and alway, even to the end of the world; and whose coming we are taught by Scripture to recognize again and again in every shaking of the earth and heaven till that last coming, when the earthly life of men shall have run itself out to its close, and He shall pronounce the judgment of Heaven upon it all. The expectation is of a Lord who is at hand; at no moment far

off from us, and sure before long in one way or
another to make His presence felt.   It is an expectation which should lead us not so much to submit
and receive as to be up and doing: ' Lo he cometh;
go ye forth to meet him.'   And if Advent teaches
the whole year the lesson of expectation, Christmas
teaches it the lesson of trustful rest in One already
come.   It takes away all vague guessing about Him
whom we see not, by pointing to the life which the
Son of God lived on earth.   It makes every gift
already received a pledge of greater things to come.

We have now reached the point at which expectation meets fulfilment.   And such also is the import
of the text.   They who spoke these words were in
like manner expecting a coming King; and within a
few hours they were permitted to behold Him, for
He was already born.   They stand before us as
seekers, but seekers on the point of finding what
they sought.   And what they sought was not some
good thing which they could take into their own
keeping.   It was a Lord to worship.   They came
not to exalt themselves, but to abase themselves ;
not to take possession of a gift but to offer a gift.
And when their homage was paid and their offerings
presented, they left Him whom they had sought with
Mary, His mother, and departed for ever into their
own land.   The answer had been given to the question in which they uttered their expectation.   They
had been guided to the place where He that was
born King of the Jews was.   Whether the babe
whom they saw there was such a king as they looked
for, we cannot tell.   At the least, when they beheld

Him, they were satisfied. They fulfilled that for
which they came: they worshipped Him. Doubtless they believed that the power which now lay hid
in Him would some day and somehow come forth
and prove Him to be a King indeed, a King over
Israel and beyond Israel; and this hope they bore
back with them to the far land from which they
came. To us, alike in their coming, their worship,
and their departure, they have left the example of
a marvellous faith, even such a faith as Christmas
demands and Christmas satisfies.

Such, in few words, is the general teaching of the
whole story, as it offers itself to us at Christmas
rather than at Epiphany. Let us now go back
and consider the text itself a little more closely.
The expectation of the wise men, dim as it might
be as to the exact shape of fulfilment, was clear
enough at least on three points: it was the expectation of a King, of a King of the Jews, and of a
born King of the Jews.

Why did their expectations take this form? We
could understand their longing for one who should
give them bread ; or, if they had bread enough,
should give them more gold to buy whatever would
minister to their comfort and pride; or one who,
since they cared for wisdom, should tell them hidden
things that they desired to know; or one who should
take away the sting of a guilty conscience, and set
them at peace with any higher god whom they
might have offended; or, better still, one who should
cleanse their will, and strengthen their power to live
a worthy life.   But their hope, as we read of it,

was simply in a king. The true King might indeed bestow all these benefits which we have been counting up: but that was not what came first to their minds. In hoping for a king, they hoped for one who would rule them; to whom they should do reverence, and whom, when the time came, they should obey. They felt that the first of all needs for themselves and for the whole distracted world was to be governed, to be bound together in a common work appointed by a common ruling head.

Again, it was a king of *the Jews* that they looked for. How was this? They were not Jews themselves; they were strangers to the commonwealth of Israel. Yet there was much in that strange nation, so full as it seemed of undying life, again and again buffeted and crushed, but not yet destroyed, worshipping One unseen God at one holy place with psalm and sacrifice, which might well persuade men of the East that a wondrous future was in store for Israel and the ruler of Israel. This was not the first time that Gentile witness had been borne to the divine mission of the Jewish people: twice, at two great moments of the history, a voice from the world without had done homage to the holy race. Before the Promised Land was entered, Balaam the prophet of Moab had confessed the new power that was growing in the East: " God hath brought him forth out of Egypt: he hath as it were the strength of an unicorn; he shall eat up the nations his enemies ": " I shall see him, but not now; I shall behold him, but not nigh: there shall come a Star out of Jacob, and a Sceptre shall rise out of Israel and shall smite

the corners of Moab, and destroy all the children of
Sheth." Once again, the second birth of the people
out of their long captivity was helped and blessed
by a king of the Gentile East, when Cyrus proclaimed that the Lord God of heaven had charged
him to build Him an house in Jerusalem, which is
in Judah, and sent forth the summons, "Who is
there among you of all his people? The Lord his
God be with him and let him go up."

Since that day no king of the old line had been
known in Israel. Imperfect kings of one sort or
another there had been, and there were still. But
the priestly character, which the words of Cyrus fix
on the people at large, is stamped on their whole
after history. Now however the time was come
when a true King of the Jews should arise once more
for the sake of other nations as well as His own.
Balaam had beheld and blessed a Conqueror of
enemies. That was a true vision, but an imperfect
one. Cyrus had blessed the worshippers of the God
of heaven, that broad heaven which looks down
alike on all the children of men. The later prophets
of Israel had been led by the Spirit to declare the
God of Israel to be the God of all the ends of the
earth. No wonder then, if, when the time was ripe,
wise men of the East, looking forward to a coming
King, looked for Him in the midst of that one
people who had learned and cherished the secret
of converse with the Most High. They had no fear
that this King of the Jews would treat Gentiles like
themselves as mere enemies to be conquered. A
king who would not seek his subjects' good was

far enough from their thoughts. That he should
rule them was what they desired and what they
did not fear. If Israel, in the counsels of heaven,
was ordained to be the bearer of life and light to
other nations, then they would think it no disgrace
but a joy to do homage to Israel and Israel's Lord.

Once more the wise men asked for Him that
was *born* King of the Jews. How they supposed
that this could be at that time we know not: many
thoughts were doubtless possible then which do not
occur to us now. But the word assuredly meant
at least thus much, that the expected King was
not one raised to his throne by his own right hand,
or by the voice of men, for his strength or courage
or wisdom or riches, but one carrying a divine title
from his birth. That King was not to be a Saul,
not even a David, but a David's son. There was
another king in the land already, Herod the king,
as the Bible calls him, a powerful ruler, cruel and
unscrupulous, but magnificent in his doings, the very
ruler to draw to him men of the East with the
charm of awe. He was no true Jew, much less of
David's line; there was nothing in him of the true
Jew's heart, which was David's heart. Many of his
own subjects might be dazzled by the one who promised to make them strong with earthly strength,
because they were indifferent to his readiness to
profane all that their fathers had kept holy. But
to the wise men he could never be what they sought.
They took no sort of account of him as they entered
Jerusalem, asking, "Where is he that is born King
of the Jews?"

The question was asked by *them*, as we have seen, in hopeful expectation. But the words will bear another meaning. They could be spoken, they were virtually spoken, by others in terror, and again in scorn. The terror is recorded in the next verse. First, there is the terror of Herod. He was troubled, we read, when he heard these words. His trouble led him to ask a like question. He inquired where the Christ, the long-looked for Messiah, was expected to be born. Till then he had no suspicion that one was arising, or arisen, who had higher claims than his own. Even now how slight was the proof! Some strangers from a distant land had come asking a question and telling of a star: and that was all. Yet still he was troubled, and his terror found vent in the murder of the children of Bethlehem. He had on his side all that men count strength. Already he had destroyed many a real or fancied rival. He had possession, a powerful army, a full treasury, the fear of subjects and the admiration of neighbours, the favour of mighty Rome. Yet he was troubled at an unknown infant's birth. Half unbeliever, half idolater as he was, the covenant and the hope of Israel still haunted his dreams.

But St. Matthew speaks of another terror at the wise men's question. *All Jerusalem*, he says, was troubled with Herod. Jerusalem troubled to hear of a born King of the Jews! Think what a state of things is implied in those few words. Think of the city where David and Solomon had reigned, the holy place to which the tribes went up, being thrown into fear because He whom they professed to expect was at last come, the Heir of David and of the promises made to David, the King in whom righteousness and peace should meet. Yes, but this was just what in their hearts they dreaded. A reign of righteousness and peace would break in most painfully upon their cherished ways of life. They were proud to call themselves by the name of the Lord God, proud to offer sacrifices in IIis temple, proud to guard the letter of His law and curse all who seemed to slight it. But a King close at hand who would interfere with the wars and fightings that came from the lusts in their members, and the smooth cheatings and stealings with which they hasted to be rich, and the pitiless hardness with which they ground down and, worse, despised the poor—the news of such a King was alarming indeed. Better it seemed to have a Herod with all his cruelties and oppressions, who would at least honour their religion by rebuilding and beautifying their temple, and satisfy their passion for exciting amusements by building also an amphitheatre, where they might enjoy the agonies of men fighting with wild beasts.

The terror of Herod broke into violence at once. The terror of Jerusalem was longer before it found its natural end in murder, and then it appeared to succeed where Herod had failed. From the day when Christ cleansed the temple with His scourge of small cords, Jerusalem trembled more and more with fear, and the hatred which grows out of fear. Another younger Herod and Pilate, the soldier of jealous Rome, could find no fault in Him, when at length He stood accused of owning Himself to be an anointed King. They were willing to release Him; but rulers, priests, scribes, people, all Jerusalem demanded His death. "We will not have this man to reign over us." Pilate asked, "Shall I crucify your king?" and Jerusalem answered, "We have no king but Cæsar."

On that same day the leading words of the text were set in another light. We have heard of the terror of Herod and Jerusalem; let us dwell now for a moment on the scorn of Pilate. Outside the walls of Jerusalem the middle cross bore the writing, "Jesus of Nazareth, the King of the Jews." Had that short, contemptuous title been lengthened out into a sentence, we could fancy its becoming this very question: "*Where* is He that is born King of the Jews? Where is He now? Look, proud Jews, ye who count yourselves the holiest of mankind, see where your own King hangs in death, and shame worse than death." Surely the taunt was natural. The answer to it could not yet be given; nay, it could never be given by those for whom it was meant. But it is for us to mark how He who was born King of the Jews died as King of the Jews, and was proclaimed as such before all eyes, not only in Hebrew, the one sacred language of the Jewish past, but in Greek and Latin, the twin sacred languages of the world-wide future. Other names, greater names than this, are His; but to the end of time He remains what the worshipping wise men and the mocking Pilate called Him, the King of the Jews.

Once more we seem to catch a faint echo of the wise men's question a generation or two later, again in a tone unlike theirs. The period had begun to which we too, brethren, belong—the age of waiting for the return of our ascended Lord. Men soon grew weary of waiting. They asked some in scorn, some no doubt in honest, helpless perplexity, "Where is the promise of His coming? Where is that King now?" The finger no longer points to a visible cross with a visible body hanging upon it, but into the blank air. The suggested answer is no longer that the King of Israel has come to shame and death, but that He has melted into nothingness. Where shall we find for ourselves the true way to meet such questions when they rise in our hearts? How shall we keep our Advent from being a mere expectation with nothing to sustain it, or else an expectation full only of terror and troubling, and at last of hatred? Christmas gives the answer, or rather the beginning of an answer, in which each great season of the Christian year has its part. Between Bethlehem and the Mount of Ascension the gospel story supplies the one firm assurance that the anointed Lord is nigh. But the assurance comes with especial power from that early page of the story which is opened to us to-day. Bethlehem rebukes our slackness to recognize the marks of the invisible King's presence now, and to look forward confidently to His triumph, by setting before us the small and obscure beginnings, nay, we may say the very nothingness, out of which in due time came forth His career of redemption. In the darkness of that night on which Christ was born no glory shone round His immediate presence. To faith alone God granted some measure of light and of guidance from above, to the faith of Jewish shepherds and the faith of wise men from the East.   Only the patient guardians of the flocks could see the glory from above, and hear the angel's message and the song of the heavenly host.   The single star among the countless hosts of the sky revealed itself only to eyes that watched and waited.   The outer world saw no light in the darkness.   This is a true image of the whole course of things.   No token of Godhead attended the birth or infancy or childhood.   Not till the baptism did the Father proclaim from heaven, " This is my beloved Son, in whom I am well pleased."   Not till after the baptism was the power to do mighty works put forth.   Born in a village known only for the equally obscure birth of a great king long ago, bred in a remote district whose name was a bye-word of contempt, the King of Israel gave no outward sign of His royalty.   Emptiness, lowness, feebleness surrounded Him who was able at last to say, "All power is given unto me in heaven and earth."

To return once more to the words of the text, the question of the wise men recalls some shortcomings in our ordinary thoughts which cannot but mar our lives.   We find it hard to attach any clear sense to the Bible when it puts Christ before us as a King; still harder to believe that His kingship is part of the glad tidings of great joy.   The reason is because we fail to see that our first and greatest need is to have some one to reverence and to obey. The whole world needs this, every set of men needs

it, every one of us separately needs it.   To do that
which is right in our own eyes is to be under a
curse, a debasing slavery in the guise of freedom.
Our King Himself went through the same discipline
in this respect which is appointed for us.   The
child's first lesson of obedience was His first lesson.
His subjection to His mother and to Joseph, who
was called His father on earth, is clearly written
in the Gospel.   When that subjection grew looser,
it was not that He might become, as we should
say, His own master, but that He might devote
Himself more completely to doing the will of His
Father in heaven, and being occupied about *His*
work.

Nor has His title, "King of the Jews," lost
its force for us men of the West.   It marks not
only the never-ceasing debt of all mankind in the
past to the holy nation whose were the law and
the prophets, and of whom as concerning the flesh
the Christ came.   It sets forth a truth respecting
Himself, true now and always, which is sorely needed
for a right knowledge of His Person and Work.
And again it reminds us that God's best gifts to
mankind still go forth through an Israel, His new
Israel, His Church universal.   The Prince of all the
kings of the earth is before all things the Head of
the Church.   Christian people fall easily into one
of two errors.   Either they forget that Christ died
for the whole world and rules the whole world, not
the Church only; or else they practically leave out
the Church altogether from their faith as Christians
and their thoughts about ordinary life.   Scripture

on the other hand teaches us, partly by the example
of Israel, partly by the express words of Christ and
His Apostles, how it is God's will to use His Church
as His leading instrument for carrying out His work
of healing and blessing among all mankind. The
privilege of knowing our King and worshipping Him
is given us, not for our own sakes only, but also for
the sake of those who know Him not or acknowledge Him not.

But does the Church indeed confess Him for its
Head, and take His work in all its length and
breadth as the pattern of its own work? Would it
not be only too easy for strangers from afar, wise
men from the East, to see in Christendom only a
headless rabble, dragged hither and thither by jealousies and self-seekings, anything rather than united
in the sense of a common obedience and a common
labour? Can it be that, if they came among us
asking in all anxious sincerity, "Where is He that
is born Lord of the Church?" we should be found,
like Jerusalem, trembling at the mention of His
name, dreading nothing so much as His immediate
presence among us, preferring any Herod who will
enrich us or feed us or amuse us, to a righteous
Lord who demands righteousness in His people?
This is a question which, even at this happy season,
every congregation, representing as it must among
its own surroundings the Church universal in the
midst of the world, should ask itself; and which
each one of us should ask himself, that he may
learn to recognize and confess his own share in that
which is the concern of all.

To see our true Lord clearly now, to discern the mighty workings of His kingdom overcoming the sin and folly of men which resist it, is often hard in the darkness of our imperfect vision. Yet if we will but look for it, we shall always find some star of His risen in the East to give promise of His coming, and to guide us to where we may worship Him and obey Him. Then in due time worship and obedience will bring their own reward in increase of light and yet greater increase of love. The partial knowledge of faith grows into the perfect knowledge of full communion. The Babe of Bethlehem conducts us to the Father's right hand in heaven.

IV

GOD MAKING ALL THINGS NEW

Great Saint Mary's Church, before the University. Christmas Day, 1889.

" AND I heard a great voice out of the throne saying, Behold, the tabernacle of God is with men, and he shall dwell with them, and they shall be his peoples, and God himself shall be with them and be their God. And he shall wipe away every tear from their eyes; and death shall be no more: neither shall there be mourning nor crying nor pain any more: the first things are passed away. And he that sitteth on the throne said, Behold, I make all things new."—*Rev.* xxi. 3-5 (R.V.).

THE first words which St. John heard uttered by the great voice out of the throne contain, under forms of speech carried on from the Old Testament, the simplest message of Christmas. By that tabernacling of God with men, which we commemorate to-day, we have sure knowledge of His perpetual presence and kingdom among mankind: and by that same faith of Christmas we learn to interpret that banishing of sorrow and death of which the voice goes on to give assurance.

On neither of these two themes do I propose to speak expressly to-day, but only on the· third, to which they both lead, the utterance of Him that sat

on the throne.   Yet, while we listen to that word of
His, it is well that the earlier verses should still be
lingering in our ears.   The Christmas joy renewed
year by year, and that sorrow which is filling all our
hearts to-day,[1] are here joined together in one divine
strain.

"Behold, I make all things new."   These are
words which at once compel attention.   Feelings
of some sort or other are stirred up in the mind
of every one when they are spoken in his hearing.
They come home in one way or other to the every-
day thoughts of every human being.   It matters not
whether he cares for God or not ; it matters not
whether he cares for his fellow-creatures or even for
his family and his friends or not ; it matters not
whether he uses his mind upon any object that
comes before him, or lives a wholly senseless and
unreflecting animal life.   Be he as selfish or as dull
of heart as he may, there must be in him either
gladness or distress to hear of all things being made
new.   Quite indifferent he cannot be.

Let us consider a little who they are that will be
repelled by the thought of things being made new.
First, those who are prosperous themselves, and do
not distress themselves, and are heedless of the lot of
others.   There is nothing like *comfort* for causing
this fear of what is new.   To have no serious care
about daily bread, to be able to make a certain and
a sufficient living by a fair and moderate amount of
familiar labour, or perhaps without any labour, and
when work is over to have abundance of easy enjoy-

[1] Dr. Lightfoot, Bishop of Durham, died December 23rd, 1889.

ment,—this is the kind of life which makes men desire that all things should remain just as they are.

But there is also a nobler kind of dread of new things. Most men, when they have lived a certain time in one place, throw out roots, as it were, all round them, and attach themselves to everything in the midst of which they are habitually dwelling. The house in which they live, the church perhaps in which they worship, the streets or fields among which they walk, in short all their daily and weekly surroundings become in a manner a part of their very selves. It is impossible to alter anything near them without sending a quiver through them as though it were the wounding of a limb. Every breach of custom offends them as a violence done to a divine order. If they find *many* things becoming new, they are bewildered as though an earthquake were rocking the ground under their feet.

This dread of newness, unlike the first, has in it nothing base. There is no wisdom, not even any solid and enduring strength when it is wholly wanting. Yet we all know how often it will lead us astray. Not to speak of the correction of manifest evils, things good may often need to be changed for better. Things good to *us* may often need to be taken away because they are not good to others, whose claims to be considered are stronger than ours. In these and various other ways it is often a duty to welcome change : but that is a duty which we can never understand so long as we look upon long-standing custom as the one only holy thing in the world.

Once more there are those who hate the prospect of new things, neither from dull selfishness nor from an affectionate clinging to the familiar ways of their own past life, but because they are soberly and deliberately convinced that change brings more evils than it cures. They see clearly that most certain truth, that it is easier to destroy than to create, and that the best and most precious things are of slow growth. And so, for the sake of mankind no less than of themselves, they would rather put up with a few old miseries than be plunged into a flood of change which may carry men they know not whither.

Here then, brethren, there are three classes of men, to each of which some in at least every educated congregation belong, to whom the announcement of all things being made new can have only a threatening sound. They find it hard to understand how it is possible for any one of sober and serious mind to rejoice at it. Yet assuredly there are many who delight in the prospect. And on this side too the motives are of differing worth. Some will welcome change out of nothing better than childish giddiness, glad to see things turned upside down for the mere sport, at bottom caring for the new no more than for the old. Others, a vast host, will be gladdened by the promise of a new order of things, because the present state bears so hardly, so cruelly, upon themselves; and life is to them so full of bitter toil or care or sorrow that they are sure almost any change must be for the better. Others again, not themselves the victims of a hard fate, but feeling deeply for those who

are, can see nothing but hope for mankind in every
thing that breaks in upon old established custom, and
opens the way to fresh manners of life. No doubt
there are many who glibly speak in this way out of
empty imitation, or worse out of envy or hatred or
the subtle lust of destructiveness. But no less true
is it that many of the best of our fellow-creatures
believe strongly that long continuance in one state
leads surely to decay and death, and look forward to
frequent and vigorous change as the best assurance of
welfare for all. How can they then do otherwise
than welcome One who declares the making new
of all things as a messenger of good tidings indeed?

This opposition of old and new enters deeply into
all our thoughts when we have *any* thoughts. It
constantly rules our actions even without our knowledge, if no stronger impulse of the moment is present
to overmaster it. It might seem then that a message
like this from the text could not possibly bring comfort or joy to all of us alike, whether we desired
change or feared it. Yet assuredly it can, though it
may be that we all alike have much to learn before
we can be fit to receive it. No one who reads the
passage as it occurs in the book of Revelation can
doubt that the voice which said " Behold, I make all
things new," was intended chiefly to declare glad
tidings, and thus it seems to give divine consent
to those who cannot be content that things should
remain as they are. So in truth it does : yet we
must not hastily read in it a rebuke to those who
fear to snap any thread which joins them to their
forefathers or to their own former selves. The

message is a true gospel from God, but for that
very reason it has within it much more than a bare
echo of any thoughts of our own hearts. All good
news that truly comes from God not merely gladdens
but teaches and purifies. In part it meets the natural
desires which spring up within us ; in part it changes
them, and glorifies them into desires of a loftier and
wiser sort. When then we hear God saying to us
" Behold, I make all things new," we must not be
content with bringing His word down to our own
hopes or our own fears : we must try to understand
it if we can in the light of *His* great counsels as the
Lord of all, and so our hopes and fears will be lifted
up into a world of light : we shall not be bidden to
unlearn them, but we shall be taught to correct their
ignorances, and in so doing shall find them stronger
and wider.

First, it is well to remember the time at which the
words were written down. According to the date
best attested by the internal evidence of the book
itself, the Revelation came to St. John in a time of
the utmost danger to the Church, between the years
when the other Apostles were living and the later
years in which St. John stood alone. Jew and
heathen were at last united in hatred to the name
of Christ, and were putting forth all their power to
destroy those who believed in Him. St. James, St.
Peter, St. Paul had lately passed to their heavenly
home through the gate of a glorious death. The
fall of the holy city was close at hand. The old
memorials of God's presence were vanishing from
the earth. They whom from of old He had chosen

to be His own people were being cast away and scattered upon the face of the world. Death and hell were riding triumphant over everything that was marked with God's name. Change was come in its most terrible form, as sheer destruction, destruction most of all of that which was best of all. Then it was, when God seemed to be deserting the earth, that a great voice was heard out of the throne saying, "'Behold, the tabernacle of God is with men, and he shall dwell with them, and they shall be his peoples, and God himself shall be with them and be their God. And he shall wipe away every tear from their eyes; and death shall be no more; neither shall there be mourning, nor crying, nor pain any more ; the first things are passed away.' And He that sitteth on the throne said, ' Behold, I make all things new.'" The first heaven and the first earth were passed away : a new heaven and a new earth could already be seen by one whose eyes God opened. But behind the new heaven and the new earth was He who made them; and what, when He Himself spoke, He announced as His work was the work of making all things new.

What came of that work of God we all partly know. The new heaven under which men have lived ever since is the heaven of the gospel of Christ, the vision and recognized presence of God as made known in the life, death, and resurrection of His only begotten Son. To St. John himself in his late old age was committed the task of guiding our eyes to that new heaven by the image of Christ, which he has set before us in his Gospel. The new earth is the earthly life now redeemed and glorified in the flesh and blood of the Son of Man. The old Jewish heaven and Jewish earth are gone, because such was the will of Him who makes all things new.

But it is needful to look at God's manner of making new. Sometimes, as at that time, the change comes with a mighty destruction and the crack of doom. But has the old really perished? Is anything that was precious in the earth or the heaven of the old time taken clean away out of our reach? The answer lies in the Bibles which we hold in our hands. They have an Old Testament as well as a New. Adam's earth is ours. David's heaven is ours. Israel after the flesh has grown into Israel after the spirit. We cannot neglect the Scriptures of the Old Covenant without misreading the Scriptures of the New Covenant. It was Christ's coming that made the law to cease, and rendered useless part at least of the office of the prophets. Yet Christ Himself said, " Think not that I came to destroy the law, or the prophets : I came not to destroy, but to fulfil." That in them which He did seem to destroy had, in fact, already died a natural death, for its work was done ; but in making all things new He brought life and immortality into the old. And even so must they in each generation strive to act who follow in His steps.

Such is the lesson from the days of the Revelation of St. John. It comes to us again in another form when we give the words the widest range, and understand them of God's whole government of the world. For verily He is *always* making all things

new. Even when the course of the world is very
quiet and seems to be at a standstill, He is but
changing the manner of this His work, for some
of His most wonderful renewals are wrought in
silence. He is Himself described as He that sitteth
on the throne. The words refer us back no doubt to
an earlier verse, and that again to a series of passages
throughout the book, but assuredly they carry their
own force with them here. The image, as it is truly
set before us for the first time in the Revised Version
(not " he that sat " but " he that sitteth "), is of calm
unchanging majesty, abiding through all the swiftly
shifting scenes of prophetic vision. He rules, but
rests as He rules. The Author of unceasing change,
He knows no change within Himself. He is older
than the oldest things, His name is the Ancient
of days. The old and the new have thus alike
their perfect pattern in Him. His counsels partake
of both : on the one hand they stand fast from age
to age, on the other they are ever advancing from
step to step by new births of time.

In what spirit, it is surely well to ask, are *we*
looking forward to the coming time? Are we dreading every change as though it must abolish all that
we care to live for? Then we can have no faith
in the God who reveals Himself to us as making
all things new. Are we ready to cast to the winds
all old things which do not directly serve our own
profit and comfort, and eager only for the novelty of
an untried world? Then we can understand little of
the things which make up the true riches of men.
But if we learn to think of Him as belonging alike

to the old and the new, we shall gladly go forward,
and gladly take Him for our Guide as we go.   All
His mighty works of old will be pledges of the
mightier works which He is ready to accomplish
in the ages yet unborn.   According to our faith He
does unto us.   If we trusted Him more, we should
find ourselves lifted up by a mightier force, whether
to do or to endure.   His past deeds, and most of all
the deeds which He wrought in His Son Jesus, are
the food on which our faith must be sustained ; and,
if it is a faith indeed, we shall know that He will
never forsake either ourselves or any good cause in
which we are enlisted, since all are part of His
eternal plan.

But how is such a faith to be attained ?   If we
are used to living as though God were only a
venerable name, how shall we set Him and keep
Him in the very front of our thoughts ?   Here is
the very question which more than all others is
answered for each man's own heart by the promise
which these words of the text convey.   The better
we know, the more we grieve over our own spiritual
deadness, the more hopeless will it seem to find
any way of recovery.   The old gains such terrible
mastery over us that we may well despair of finding
an entrance for the new.   All our past history has
left its mark upon body and mind.   We cannot but
feel ourselves enslaved to that which we have made
ourselves.   Habits that once were young and weak,
and might have been broken, have grown into rigid
stubbornness, and we are helpless against their
tyranny.   It is hard for us to even desire in earnest

to be changed ; desiring it, it is harder still to make
any progress towards anything deserving the name.
But He who sits on the throne speaks and says to
us, "Behold, I make all things new," yea, all things,
even hearts set fast in old hardness and perversion.
His promise of a new heart and a new spirit is
the most difficult of all to believe as soon as we
have come to know what the words mean.   It
cannot be fulfilled till we learn to sink ourselves
utterly in Him.   And then His way of changing
the old into the new meets us once more.   It is
not a new character that He gives us, but a new
spirit.   The new grows out of the old ; all that
is fit for His service He preserves and fits for better
uses, and suffers no true gain of our own past to
be lost.

> " Eternal growth hath no dull fears,
>   But freshening still with seasons past,
>   The old man clogs its earlier years,
>   And simple childhood comes the last."

V

ST. JOHN THE EVANGELIST

St. Ippolyts, St. John the Evangelist's Day, 1868.

"THAT which we have seen and heard declare we unto you, that ye also may have fellowship with us."—1 *John* i. 3.

WE are still in the midst of Christmas. The taking of our human nature by the Son of God, and the birth at Bethlehem through which His earthly life began, are the great facts which should still be ruling our hearts when we come before God to worship Him. But in the services of to-day another name is added to Christ's. We are bidden to give God thanks for St. John the Evangelist, the Apostle who wrote the last Gospel. He, the disciple whom Jesus loved, who leaned on Jesus's breast as they sat at that strange Passover feast the night before the Crucifixion—he is brought within the blaze of the divine glory. We are encouraged to strengthen and enlarge our thoughts of Christmas by mixing them with thoughts of that chosen disciple.

St. John has a double claim to be remembered at

this season; for what he was to Christ, and for what he is to us. What he was to Christ I have already reminded you: what he is to us in the writings from his hand which we are blest in being able to read, we shall know better and better every year of our lives if we cherish any love for his Lord and ours. His book of Revelation, his Epistles, and most of all his Gospel, speak to us as though he were bodily present among us, and set before us in ever-growing and uprising light the Lord of glory whom we are perpetually forgetting. The image stamped upon *his* soul is the clearest and most abiding assurance we have that God's Holy One did indeed once walk upon this earth in our shape, died our death, and by rising again bestowed upon us the gift of His own life. Thus the two reasons why we should remember him before God with grateful honour meet together into one. It was his very nearness to Jesus of Nazareth which enabled him to be to us the mouthpiece of the brightest, the deepest, the most everlasting Gospel.

Let us try to gather up the leading points of his life and character as they are to be found in the New Testament. The first trace of him is in the thirty-fifth and following verses of the first chapter of his own Gospel, where, though not named, he is easily to be recognized. He appears there as one of John the Baptist's disciples. Like so many others of the better part of the nation, he had obeyed the call to repentance, and joined himself to the bold preacher who was labouring to rouse a careless and sinful people out of their dangerous slumber. He and Andrew were standing by John the Baptist's side when they saw Christ walk before them, as yet unknown by any wonderful words or works. But John the Baptist's eye could yet discern the divine Spirit that was in Him, and his words, " Behold the Lamb of God," were not lost on the two disciples. They followed Jesus; and when He turned and said, " What seek ye? " they answered, " Master, where dwellest thou? " He replied, in words which now sound like a prophecy of the whole Gospel history, " Come and see." And they came and saw where He dwelt, and abode with Him that day. That day for the first time John dwelt where Jesus dwelt, and so the foundation was laid of that familiarity with the deepest secrets of life and love, which has made St. John's writings the richest treasure of the human race.

It would seem to have been a long while after that day before they met again. After John the Baptist was cast into prison, we read in St. Mark's first chapter, Jesus came into Galilee preaching the gospel of the kingdom of God. And there, as He walked beside the lake, He found John pursuing his trade as a fisherman along with his brother James. He bade them come after Him and follow Him, and from that day they took their share in the work of preaching and healing which He carried on nearly to His death. John the Baptist's work was now over. God had laid him aside, and was soon to take him to Himself. To have been *his* disciple was the best imaginable apprenticeship for becoming Christ's disciple, and that was the privilege of our St. John.

Once upon a time, while he was still looking up to the Baptist as his highest earthly leader, he had been constrained to follow the Lamb of God for a few brief hours. Now, without any forsaking of his old master, he had found a yet higher service; and henceforth he was one of those who follow the Lamb whithersoever He goeth. He was one of the twelve whom Christ named Apostles, His own special companions whom at times He sent where He could not go Himself. But more than this, he was one of the three admitted to a closer intimacy. At the raising of Jairus' daughter, on the mountain at the time of the meeting with Moses and Elijah in glory, and in the garden during the great agony he, along with his brother St. James and with St. Peter, was permitted to enter within the holy ground, while others were kept out at a distance.

If, on the other hand, we put together the few signs which we possess of St. John's own character at this time, the result is rather surprising. From various causes, but chiefly because we often hear St. John called the Apostle of love, and because we have such silly and feeble notions of what love really is, we are apt to think of St. John as a soft womanish kind of man. It is not so that he appears in the Gospels. To him and to his brother our Lord gave the name "Sons of Thunder." And so it was they who wished to call down fire from heaven on the Samaritan village which refused to receive Christ on His way to Jerusalem; and it was John in particular who was angry that devils should be cast out because it was not done in Christ's name.

Yet these marks of passionate zeal, which drew
down stern rebukes from the Lord, in whose honour
they appeared to be ·displayed, were but perversions
of a great and noble character not yet come to
ripeness. This example teaches us how grievously
mistaken we are when we take credit for meaning
no harm and doing no harm, and persuade ourselves
that that is something to be very proud of. What
endeared St. John so deeply to Him who knew what
was in man was this burning eagerness to hate and
crush the evil, and to pursue and lay hold on the
good; and for the sake of that rare and precious
eagerness the faults of rash and ill-timed passionate-
ness were easily forgiven.

When Christ stood a prisoner before the earthly
priest and the earthly king, He stood alone. All
the disciples had forsaken Him and fled, St. John
among the rest. The sudden terror of the soldiers
in the dark night, with their torches and weapons,
the knowledge of the deadly hatred of the Jews who
had sent them, were too much for his still imperfect
faith. But there was a speedy return from that
shameful desertion. St. John, with St. Peter, loitered
about the house where the trial was going on. He
stood by the cross where his Master hung a-dying.
Then it was that the words were spoken which, if
we consider them well, show more strikingly than
any others what St. John was to Christ, and what
Christ was to St. John. "When Jesus," we read,
"saw his mother and the disciple standing by, whom
he loved, he saith unto his mother, ' Woman, behold
thy son.' Then saith he to the disciple, ' Behold thy·

mother.' And from that hour that disciple took her unto his own home."

We can see at once what a solemn charge was contained in the words. To be entrusted for life with the care of his Lord's mother was the highest mark of confidence that any disciple could receive at such a time. And the words in which the charge was conveyed spoke even more. They were in fact the adoption of St. John as in the strictest sense a brother, and a command to Mary to look upon him henceforth as she had looked upon the Holy Child of her womb. But this wonderful joining together of St. Mary and St. John does in fact point to the mysterious privileges which they each enjoy, and share with no other. She, the humble handmaid of the Lord, whom all generations shall call blessed, was the only member of the family of Nazareth, the household of His childhood, whom Jesus could acknowledge for His own at that last hour. Her husband Joseph was doubtless dead; Christ's brothers, that is probably Joseph's children, did not believe in Him. But the tie which bound Him to the mother who bore Him He never so distinctly honoured as at that awful time when the salvation of the world was being accomplished: and it is impossible to imagine a higher honour set upon ties of blood than this intermingling of their duties with the Redeemer's self-sacrifice for all mankind.

And what St. Mary is among kinsfolk, that and even more than that is St. John among friends. Others beside him were loved and trusted by Jesus, loved not merely as He loved all men but as friends, companions of His daily doings. John, however, I say, is evidently much more. He was the friend of Christ's own special choice, the one with whom we feel that Christ in the strictest sense lived in communion, a communion on both sides of giving and of receiving. He was indeed the friend who sticketh closer than a brother, and who was admitted to a holy trust for which brothers were found unworthy. And here again it is a blessed thing to find the highest honour put upon friendship of this kind, upon the intimacy which comes by choice no less than upon the intimacy which comes by blood. But yet more blessed is it, and a true Christmas blessing, to have these clear and unfailing signs of the reality of Christ's having indeed taken upon Him our nature, when we learn how deeply the sense of the closest kinship and the closest friendship wrought in Him during those solemn moments when the widest counsels of the Most High God were being fulfilled.

The fruits of that peculiar honour granted to St. John were to appear in due time; but not for many a long year. The foremost man in the infant Church was not to be St. John but St. Peter. These two old friends are to be seen together again on the morning of the Resurrection, running to visit the tomb which Mary Magdalene had found empty. They were together at the last draught of fishes some days later, and the prophetic conversation which followed, part of which we read in the Gospel for to-day. In Acts iii. and iv. we find them going up together into the temple; imprisoned together, and brought together before the council. After that St. John vanishes almost wholly from sight, except in his own writings. No doubt during all these years he laboured constantly and successfully for the good of the Church. But, as far as we can see, he must have laboured only as one among the Apostles, and his power must have been sunk in the general life of the Christian body. His own proper time was not yet come.

The services of yesterday were in honour of St. Stephen the martyr, the first Christian who was killed for being a Christian. St. John suffered the martyrdom of banishment, but not of death. But it was through martyrdom that he was raised at last to his high calling. We read in the Acts how his own brother James was put to death by Herod, and the memory of that sorrow and that glory must have burned for ever after in his soul. But at length days of fierce persecution came upon the whole Church. St. Peter and St. Paul were slain by the heathen at Rome ; St. James, the Lord's repentant brother, was slain by the Jews at Jerusalem. Multitudes of nameless Christians suffered death by cruel torments. Every race of men alike was turned against the helpless believers in the Crucified. It seemed as if the Christian name must shortly be trampled out of the world. Then in that great and terrible day of the Lord, when nation was rising against nation, and kingdom against kingdom, John beheld visions in his lonely banishment, and that book of Revelation, of which we read the first and the last chapters to-day,[1] preserves for us his divine

[1] Viz., according to the Old Lectionary.

pictures of the great warfare which is ever being
waged between God and His enemies, and of the
heavenly city of peace which lies beyond. This was
the beginning of St. John's gifts to the Church. The
thought of martyrdom, of bearing witness for God
and His Christ, runs through the whole book : it is
all a prophecy out of the midst of sore anguish.
That time of trouble did not pass quickly away.
When Jerusalem itself was destroyed, God's kingdom
on earth might well appear to be shaken to its
foundation. The Church had no longer a holy city,
a visible seat of the Most High. Though persecution ceased and quiet days came back, Christian
hearts might well be in sore doubt and dismay, not
knowing whither to turn. Dangers from within
sprang up in place of dangers from without. The
faith of Christ was denied by those who still called
themselves by His name. Faith, hope, charity, and
wisdom were as much needed as in time of blood-
shed, and far harder to be found.

The one link which joined the Church of that
time to the days before the great persecution was
the Apostle St. John. It was probably through his
wisdom under God's guidance that the worst dangers
were escaped, and the faith of Christ lived on. His
Gospel and his Epistles are the record of his labour,
and themselves contain the message which he wished
to hand down to later generations. They are full of
new thoughts, reaching beyond anything which we
can find in the earlier books of the New Testament.
But the foundation of all that he has to say lies in
his recollection of the words and works of the Lord.

He felt that the only sure way to keep the Church
from falsehood and folly was to do his best to set up
before it the image of the divine Saviour, which dwelt
so surely in his own heart. If he could only make
them know Jesus of Nazareth as he had known
Him, he felt they would have an unfailing key to
open every difficulty that might arise. This is the
strain of the text, as it is of the whole First Epistle
and the Gospel. "That which *we* have seen and
heard declare we unto you, that ye also may have
fellowship with us." And with this purpose the
Gospel was written, as a better and safer guide to
truth than the wisest arguments.

As we read those last few verses of the Gospel
which we heard this morning, we seem to see the
lonely old man looking back over half an ordinary
lifetime to the day when Peter was allowed to glorify
God by a death like his Master's on the cross, and
he was left by himself to fight the Master's battle
without human help or counsel. But his eye dwells
on that day only for a moment. His gaze rests
steadily on a time, a whole ordinary lifetime back, a
time which lasted only a few months, though it now
appears as if he could never come to the end of all
that was contained in them. The words and deeds
of the Son of God rise up before his memory with a
distinctness wanting in all the years between. As
he sits and writes, wonderful sayings till now forgotten come forth from unknown chambers of his
heart. What was confused and dim at the time is
now made bright and clear by the thoughts and the
sufferings of later years. It is a larger, more manifold

Christ that stands before his heart at this later age,
and, while he himself abides within the presence of
that remembered Christ, nothing appears dark to him.

We do not see these things, brethren, but St. John
saw them : and the reason why they are hidden from
us is not the want of apostolic powers, but of apostolic
holiness.   He at all events declares to us what he
has seen and heard, and shall it be said of us, " No
man receiveth his testimony"?   " These things write
we unto you," he says, " that your joy may be full."
Is the joy that we make to ourselves so very satisfying, that we can be content to live as though St.
John had never written of Christ, or Christ Himself
come ?

VI

MAN VISITED BY GOD

Emmanuel College Chapel, Epiphany, 1887.

"WHAT is man that thou art mindful of him, and the son of man that thou visitest him?"—*Psalm* viii. 4.

THESE words, or nearly these words, occur several times in the Bible with different purposes. They are not, properly speaking, a message from heaven to men, unveiling to their eyes some great glory or blessedness, or setting them some high task to be done; but they are a voice of man, thinking aloud about himself, and lifting up his dim thoughts to God above. They are a question, and yet not a question, which asks directly for an answer. They speak as if the state of man were a riddle which is not yet wholly read; but still they are taken up altogether with facts about which there can be no uncertainty, and with wonder at what is not doubted to be true. They belong to no one age or estate of life: they are equally well suited to happiness or to misery: they seem to spring from ignorance, and yet all the knowledge in the world cannot take away from their fitness. Two lessons alone they contain, which must have been somehow learned before anyone can repeat them : he must have felt his own littleness and weakness; and he must have learned that, little and weak as he is, God cares for him and visits him.

Thus far the sense is substantially the same wherever the words occur. But they are capable of being the utterance of very different moods of mind: and such is what we actually find in the Bible. Wholly unlike the Psalmist's use of them is the bitter repetition of them put into Job's mouth in a passage of chapter vii., of which we seem to hear an echo in the early part of the first lesson for this morning. Here the words are by no means an invitation to faith and thankfulness. Job, as he said himself, was here speaking in the anguish of his spirit, and complaining in the bitterness of his soul. He, more than most men, had reason to know his own weakness. The loss of all his possessions, the death of his sons and daughters, the torments of a horrible disease were all upon him. First his wife mocked him for his simpleness of heart in trusting God, and bid him curse God and die. Then his friends mocked him for *not* trusting God as they thought, telling him of the happiness of the man whom God correcteth. All this he had to bear: he could not get rid of the thought of God if he would, for it had long been a part of himself. And he could not deny that there was much truth in what his friends told him, though it did not reach down into all the depths of his misery, or enable him to endure such misery with perfect calmness. They told him he was a poor, pitiful creature by the side of God; but who could know that half so well as he? They told him that his sufferings were signs that God was visiting him, and visiting him for his good: how could he forget that all which befel him came from God, and that all God's acts are good? This very thing was the great puzzle to him: in his agony he for the moment longed that the great God would only forget him and let him alone. It is in this temper that he utters the words which are almost the same as our text: "What is man, that thou shouldest magnify him? and that thou shouldest set thine heart upon him? And that thou shouldest visit him every morning, and try him every moment? How long wilt thou not look away from me nor let me alone?" This is not the language of a man in a right and healthy state of heart, and yet we have no right to condemn Job for it. Through that bold facing of his own tempestuous thoughts lay the way to the calm into which God purposed to bring him at last.

There must surely be some here who have been often tempted to speak as Job spoke, even if they had not his courage in confessing his own bewilderment to God in the form of a piteous prayer. There must be some who have known what it is not to forget God, nay more, to be sure that He was not forgetting them, and yet to feel His dealings so hard to bear that they have longed for Him to touch them no more. If the fit goes on and takes lasting hold of us, then it may do us grievous harm by

making God's loving-kindness seem no more to us
than a barren and hollow form of words. But it
is a good thing to have the fact of His sleepless
and unwearied dealing with each one of us brought
home to our hearts at the very moment when it
is least possible to lift up ourselves in empty pride.

But there are better uses of the text than this,
both illustrated by other parts of the Bible, and also
suggested to us by other circumstances of our own
lives. Thus, it occurs again in the 144th Psalm
this morning, the tone of which is cheerful confidence in God even in the midst of great dangers.
"Blessed be the Lord my strength, who teacheth
my hands to war, and my fingers to fight. My
loving-kindness and my fortress, my high tower and
my deliverer, my shield and he in whom I trust:
who subdueth my people under me. Lord, what
is man that thou takest knowledge of him; or the
son of man that thou makest account of him? Man
is like to vanity: his days are as a shadow that
passeth away. Bow *thy* heavens, O Lord, and come
down: touch the mountains and they shall smoke.
Stretch forth thine hand from above: rescue me, and
deliver me out of great waters . . ." and so it goes
on. The Psalmist is surrounded with great dangers,
but not crushed by them. The sense of his feebleness in the midst of powerful enemies does not cast
him down. God is greater than all. He can take
firm hold on God, and then he does not fear. And
yet it is not a helpless, sluggish, idle trust that he
feels. God visits man, not merely to do mighty
acts to him or for him, but to help him to do

mighty acts himself. God has such respect unto man as to consent to be his *teacher*. " Blessed be the Lord my strength, who teacheth *my* hands to war, and *my* fingers to fight."

We have now seen, by the examples of Job and the author of the 144th Psalm, two ways in which men may be brought to ponder within themselves, and to ask God, "What is man that thou art mindful of him, and the son of man, that thou visitest him ?" Suffering in the one case, and danger in the other, were the means which God used for teaching those His faithful servants, and which He uses still to teach us the same. But the wonderful psalm from which I first read the words, the 8th, is in a different strain, quieter in its tone, and yet reaching to a still greater depth. The verse before the text carries us back to the story of the creation, which will come before us next Sunday, in the first and second chapters of Genesis. "When I consider thy heavens, the works of thy fingers, the moon and the stars which thou hast ordained : what is man that thou art mindful of him ? and the son of man, that thou visitest him ?" Perhaps we might sometimes wonder that a book so practical as the Bible should begin with the making of the outer world in which we live, and when it first speaks of man should speak of him as innocent and unfallen ; while we, for whose use the book is written, are sadly conscious how far removed we are from such a state. Certainly if those first two chapters of Genesis were nothing more than the recital of a long vanished past, they would be not only useless for us, but the saddest

E

of all histories, and their sadness would be unre-
deemed by any usefulness; we should have to seek
elsewhere for help to guide us along the way of life.
But the truth is, the beginning of the Bible in its
own way carries in itself a message of good tidings,
no less than those parts of it which were plainly
written for our comfort. That bright picture of the
created world, and of Adam and Eve in the garden,
a parable of the ever renewed present in the form of
a narrative of the past, sets before us God's purpose
for us even now. Reading that, we know how we
still stand towards the other works of God's hands.
And assuredly such guidance is not unneeded. The
thoughts of men when they look at the world and
then at themselves do not easily take a right course.
We have all need to be taught of God in this as in
everything else. Some of us who are here present
will remember the words of a great and lofty-minded
heathen in old times, who believed most strongly
that no god does or can care for man or meddle
with the affairs of men, in a word, that no god ever
visits man either for good or for evil. He gives a
list of the evils in the world, which seemed to him
to show that it came together by chance; and last
of all he complains of the state of man as lower than
that of other beings. He describes the newborn
babe as tossed on the shore of life as a shipwrecked
sailor is cast up by the waves, helpless, speechless,
only able to utter faint cries, obliged as he grows up
to wear various clothes against heat and cold and
storm, unable to protect himself without forging arms
and building strong walls; while the races of mere

animals are helpful almost from their earliest breath, and their own body supplies them with all the clothing and weapons that they need. No one can deny that such a dark and miserable view of creation as Lucretius thus holds up to us is easy and natural enough to us all. Does it not say plainly and boldly what most of us have sometimes almost dared to think? Once take away the vision of God, and a chilling darkness like this cannot but fall on the world and on man's place in the world. There is no protection from it except in the doctrine which Genesis and the psalm set before us. Genesis tells us simply what God did and does. God made the world and all that it contains, and last of all He made man in His own image, after His own likeness. Though He made man's body of the dust of the ground, He breathed into his nostrils the breath of life, and man became a living soul. And then He set him as king over all the lower creatures who had come into being before him. The 8th psalm is not a story of how the world and man were made. It is the utterance of a psalmist's thoughts about the world and man as mirrored in his own experience. He looked upon them honestly with his own eyes just as Lucretius did. He saw the same things; confusions and miseries enough among men: men sinning and suffering and struggling and dying. And round and above man he saw a rich and wonderful world, beasts of the field, and fowls of the air, and fishes of the sea; and high up, calm and distant from the strife below, the heavens with the moon and stars.

He saw the pettiness of man in the midst of the
things of the earth and the sky above the earth.
But, instead of wailing pitifully about his low estate,
and hiding himself away from the mighty Maker
of all, he bursts into a song of praise. " O Jehovah
our Lord, how excellent is thy name in all the earth ;
who hast set thy glory upon the heavens." It is
wonderful to him that God should have put such
honour upon such a creature as man, making him
to rule all other creatures, and taking him as the
object of His own thought and love. But he has
not the least doubt of the fact. Man as the friend
and servant of God no longer belongs merely to
the earth. So long as he welcomes God in whatsoever manner God may reveal Himself to him, he
need never fall into bondage to any earthly things.

These were the thoughts of a holy and upright
Jew in days gone by. But to us Christians his
words carry a new weight of meaning, as they are
brought before us afresh in the Epistle to the
Hebrews. A new light is shed on the story of
the creation by the human birth of the Son of
God in the womb of the Virgin Mary. As time
went on, the Jews, not least when they had ceased to
worship actual idols, lost the simplicity, and therefore
the reality of their faith. Man seemed to them as
helpless in an unseen world of angels and devils,
which intercepted their view of the Lord above,
as he did to others in the outward world of stars
and clouds and wild beasts. Even the Christian
Jews were liable to be led astray by fancies of the
same kind. But the writer of that epistle felt that

true servants of Christ must lift up their heads and
walk upright in the presence of God, casting away
all such fears as become only slaves. For Christ
Himself had taken *their* nature, man's nature and not
angels' nature, and all the language of the psalm
about man could be applied to Him with perfect
truth. In Him man's weakness and man's glory
met together more completely than they had ever
done before.

To know this, brethren, is our great privilege and
blessing. Our Christian calling does not cut us off
from any of the experience through which God's
servants in old times had to pass. Christ has not
preached and been crucified before our own actual
eyes. We often find it hard to picture Him to
ourselves as a real being at all. But suffering is
here, and danger is here, and the earth and the
sky are here : and all of them are as powerful in
wakening uneasy questionings within us as they were
of old. Nay, they are God's own messengers to us,
the schoolmasters by which He would bring us to
His own Son, and through Him to Himself. We
feel bitterly, it may be, our own low estate, and
often we are tempted to murmur that Almighty
God does not so order all things that we might
escape the ills of life ; and almost, like Job, to wish
that He would cease from visiting us. O *then*, dear
brethren, let us turn to our blessed Saviour's cross,
the key to that and every other riddle. Do not
let us chide God with wantonly keeping back His
power when He might deliver us by a word, seeing
that by nothing less than by His Son's death could

even He redeem His fallen children. If we think of
man as wretched, let us remember that it was that
same manhood which Christ took and bore with Him
into heaven. The cup of suffering and danger, which
is so bitter to our lips, He drained to the lowest
dregs. And, as His sufferings were the sufferings
of man, so man, every man, is crowned with *His*
glory and honour. And His highest glory came
forth in that which so often seems to us the saddest
mark of what we are, even in His death. That was
the gate of everlasting life. That shame was what
crowned Him with glory. The life of faith in His
Father not only carried Him through His passion
and death, but turned His passion and death into
the source of life to us. And, as He has shown
us what man is, so let His *mind* dwell also in us.
Let us pray God to enable us to humble ourselves as
He humbled Himself, knowing that thus it was that
God highly exalted Him, and gave Him the name
which is above every name.

VII

THE CHURCH AND ITS MEMBERS

St. Ippolyts, Second Sunday after Epiphany, 1867.

" THERE is one body, and one Spirit, even as ye are called in one hope of your calling ; one Lord, one faith, one baptism."—*Eph.* iv. 4, 5.

To-DAY, brethren, I propose to speak to you about the Church ; something also about baptism, which is the entrance into the Church. This is a great subject in itself, belonging, when rightly understood, to the first and most necessary principles of Christian faith. At each of our services we repeat the Apostles' Creed, and there, after declaring our belief in God the Father Almighty, Maker of heaven and earth, in Jesus Christ His only Son our Lord, and in the Holy Ghost, we go on to declare our belief in the Holy Catholic Church. So also in the Nicene Creed, which we repeat in the morning service after the Collect, Epistle, and Gospel, we say, in the same place, " And I believe one Catholic and Apostolic Church, I acknowledge one baptism for the remission of sins." We are not then true Christian believers unless we believe in the Church, and we cannot do that unless we know what the Church means.

But I have a special reason for wishing to say a few words to you on this subject now. You have heard read out the Bishop's notice that in about two months from this time he proposes to confirm such young persons from this parish as shall be brought to him for that purpose. You have all heard about confirmations ; you can nearly all remember other confirmations which took place three and six and more years ago. But I very much doubt whether many of you yet understand what confirmation really is. There are good reasons why I should speak to you very fully and plainly about it from this pulpit. Of course those young persons who give notice that they are willing to be confirmed will, as usual, receive private help and instruction for some weeks before the confirmation itself takes place. But that does not take away the need of public explanation ; first, because I hope that some, who would otherwise have held back, will be induced to come forward when they have heard what I have to say in church, and so learned truer thoughts about the matter than they had before. And secondly, I wish it to be seen and felt how great interest and importance the confirmation has for the whole congregation, but especially for the parents and the elder brothers and sisters of those who are now of an age to be confirmed. Much rests with *them* during the next few days. They have it in their power to supply valuable help and encouragement to those whose welfare should be most dear to them, or by their

discouragement and indifference to give them a turn
for life away from God and the things of God.

Now, it is very hard to say anything rightly
about confirmation, impossible to explain fully what
it means, unless it is first understood what baptism
is; and again baptism cannot be rightly understood
by those who are in the dark about the Church.
With that therefore we must begin, and that we
must keep in mind all through.

First let us put aside for the present two common
meanings—perhaps the two commonest meanings—
in which we use the word 'Church.' We give that
name to the house of God in which we are now met
for worship. We speak also of the Church in opposition to dissent. Both of these meanings have
much to do with our present subject, and I shall
have to return to them by-and-bye. But we must
not begin with them, otherwise we shall misunderstand the whole matter.

A form of prayer ordered to be used, and still
sometimes used before sermons, begins thus: "Ye
shall pray for Christ's Holy Catholic Church, that is,
for the whole congregation of Christian people dis-
persed throughout the world." Here is the true
account of the Church: it is the whole body of
Christian people everywhere. In the fullest sense
it takes in all Christian people that have ever lived,
though most of them have now been dead and
forgotten for hundreds of years. It takes in all
Christian people that are now living in every land
on the face of the earth, speaking all manner of
languages, worshipping God through Christ with all

manner of differences. Unlike as they may be in
the eyes of men, before God they are all one body,
bearing the one name of His only begotten Son.
This is a great thought—one that may well lift up
the heart of every single Christian. Poor or weak
or despised as he may be, he is an equal citizen of
the mighty heavenly commonwealth; he is a member of Christ's own body. "We being many are
one body in Christ, and every one members one of
another," says St. Paul in Rom. xii. He repeats the
same more strongly in 1 Cor. xii., as in these words:
"As the body is one, and hath many members, and
all the members of that one body being many are
one body; so also is Christ. For by one Spirit are
we all baptized into one body, whether we be Jews
or Gentiles, whether we be bond or free; and have
been all made to drink into one Spirit." " Now ye
are the body of Christ, and members in particular."
And so all through the chapter. But St. Paul's
doctrine on this subject may be seen best in his
Epistle to the Ephesians from which the text is
taken, which is all more or less written about the
Church, even where the word itself does not appear.
All through it he strives to make us understand that
we, many though we be, are one body, filled with
one Spirit, and that the true life which God gives us
is one which we share together.

But you will feel, and feel rightly, that we cannot
always be stretching our thoughts to this great universal Church reaching through all ages and all
lands. We need for our own use something much
nearer to ourselves than that. Only a few among

us ever hear of the doings of Christians in old times.
We do not hear very much about the doings of
Christians of our own time in other countries, or
even, it may be, in other parts of our own country.
Any church which it is worth while for us to believe
in must be a church that comes home to us, that
has its seat among us. And such, brethren, is the
Church of Christ. The life which fills the whole
fills every part. We here in our little congregation
for this parish are an image of the universal Church.
We may, if we please, take advantage of that Church
life. If we will but act on St. Paul's words about
the body and its members, if we will but believe that
we being many are one body, made one by the
Holy Spirit which dwells among us, worshipping one
Lord, believing one faith, beginning our Christian
life from one baptism, we shall find a strength, which
we cannot know while we are striving each man
only for himself, even before the throne of God.

Let me explain what I mean by some instances.
And first let us look at our religion, our thoughts
about God and our feelings towards Him. It is
often said that a man's religion lies only between his
own conscience and his God ; that no one else has
anything to do with it. This is one of those half
truths which are more dangerous than many falsehoods. It is quite true that we stand or fall by our
own state, not by that of others. One man cannot bear the sin of another. One man cannot
please God *for* another. It is also true that there
are secrets of our hearts and consciences with our
Lord into which no other living being can enter.

There is that in each of us which belongs to himself and to no other.   But it is a poor and paltry religion which tells us that we can have no converse with God except when we are shut up within ourselves.   And yet I am afraid that most of the religion among us is of that kind.

In the common business of life we cannot help seeing how much we depend upon each other.   In some things, unless we held together, we should be ruined.   With members of our own family we are drawn more closely together by ties of affection, sometimes unhappily far too loose, yet seldom wholly wanting.   That should teach us what it is to have common desires and common interests and common regrets; to rejoice, as St. Paul says, with them that rejoice, and weep with them that weep; to feel that what touches us touches them, and what touches them touches us.   But if we have learnt this lesson by our firesides, is it not shocking that we should forget all about it when we go into the presence of God and open our hearts to Him?   Ought not our first desire to be to carry along with us, as it were, before our Heavenly Father all those whom we care for, to keep them by us in our prayers, to feel God's presence wrapping us round all together?   I am sure that many who do pray at all, pray in something like this manner for those who are dearest to them.   That is a good beginning; but that is only a beginning.   It is a lesson to point them on the way towards true Christian worship, but nothing more.

The Lord's prayer is very often on our lips.

Have we ever considered that the words ' I ' and
' my ' have no place in it, while the prayers that we
make for ourselves are full of ' I ' and ' my '? The
Lord's prayer is addressed to ' *Our* Father.' After
three petitions concerning God's name, God's kingdom, and God's will, it leads us to ask for *our* daily
bread, for forgiveness of *our* sins, and for *our* deliverance from temptation. The reason of this is plain
as soon as we believe in the Church. Whoever uses
the Lord's prayer rightly, prays not for himself alone
or his own dearest relations or friends alone: he
prays for the whole Church as a member of the
Church: he cannot pray for anything for himself
without praying for it also for all the rest.

But he must not only pray *for* them but *with*
them, as a member of the same body. In this way
we find the greatest strength and help in our converse with God and our struggle against our sins.
It is good to know that, though we be alone, apart
from all other men, we are not really alone, since
God is near us in His Son, and His Holy Spirit
dwells in our heart. But it is better to know that
in a Christian land we need never feel ourselves
cut off from other men. In every effort we make
we may be cheered by thinking how others around
us are doing the same. The feeling of being in
company, of supporting and being supported by
fellow-Christians, will make thoughts of good happier and easier, and bear abundant fruit in our lives,
supplying just that heartiness and hopefulness which
it is so difficult to keep up when we believe ourselves
to be striving single-handed.

And if once the true feeling of being members of one body took possession of our religion, what a change it would make in the spirit of our every-day lives! I do not mean only that it would make us happier and better men, because it would give strength and purity to our religion. That of course is true; but much more than that is true. Think how all our dealings with each other would be changed, if we kept steadily before our minds that all our neighbours are members of Christ's body like ourselves. Think of all the things which hold us apart from each other now. Think how we are jealous of this man, because he has got something which we have not, how we hate another because perhaps he has done us once some trifling harm, and how perhaps we hate all his family for his sake. Think how often we look on most of those around us as rivals, almost as enemies, against whom we fancy ourselves obliged to keep up a struggle. Think how we secretly rejoice in the misfortunes or mortifications of others, how ready we are to think the worst when their conduct is in question, how slow to put in a kindly word or lend a helping hand, unless it be for some particular friend. I know well the temptations to all these things, how natural it is to indulge in them. These temptations would remain still, though we had a deeper sense of Church membership. The evil passions which make war in our hearts and members would still remain, would still trouble us and distract us. But how much easier it would be to resist them if we could learn to drown all our favourite reasons for separation in the one feeling that we are all alike members of the same Church, bound to forgive and forget, bound to help and cherish, bound, in one word, to love.

This is the answer—I should rather say, this is one sufficient answer—to those who tell us that simple people need know nothing about the Church, that what they want is something more practical, more fitted to improve their lives. Brethren, I am convinced that one reason why our lives so sadly need improvement is because we have so completely forgotten all about the Church. St. Paul, at all events, shows us plainly what he thought, by the way in which he makes this doctrine of the Church the foundation of his most simple and homely lessons. This you may see for yourselves if you will read over the chapters I have already mentioned, Rom. xii., 1 Cor. xii., xiii., and many parts of Ephesians. It is not a doctrine that requires any difficult strain of thought. Believe that Christ has redeemed you, believe that He means you to look upon all who are called by His name as your brothers for His sake, believe that this is an especial duty towards those brother Christians who are connected with you as members of the same parish, and, believing all this, strive constantly to feel with them and act with them as children of the same Father: and so the doctrine will be fulfilled in your hearts and lives.

But if the belief is easy to the understanding, it is difficult to our unruly hearts. If Christ is nothing to us, how can the members of His body be any-

thing to us?   The spirit of Church membership will
ennoble our commonest actions; but it has its own
source only in our religious life. We shall never treat
our neighbours as brother Christians on week-days if
we do not worship with them on Sundays, or if we
do. not remember and rejoice in their presence while
worshipping together.   It is therefore with good
reason that the house of God bears the same name
as the congregation, and is likewise called the
church.   *We*, brethren, are the true Church, the living
Church, a part of that great Church of which Christ
is the corner-stone.   The mere building of stones
and mortar has its honour, partly because it is set
apart as a mark of God's presence among us men,
but partly also because it is the shell which holds
together the congregation of Christian men, and for
this reason takes their name, and is itself known as
the church.   It is by meeting here that we remind
ourselves before God that we are indeed members of
a divine body.   As single Christians we might worship God each in his own house, as I trust we most
of us do.   Our coming together here means that
we wish likewise to join in common prayer, in
united worship.   For this reason all our public
religious acts are performed here.   Here we meet
together in Holy Communion round Christ's table to
receive together the signs of His death, by which He
made us all one.   Here we celebrate each principal
act in the life of each of our members.   Here he is
brought to the font and admitted to be one of our
number.   Here by marriage he becomes the head of
a new family, and is united to another in the closest

bonds that are known to men in this earthly life.
Here, when he dies, his fellow-Christians meet before
they solemnly commit his body to the ground as
that of a dear brother, and mingle their hopes of a
joyful resurrection with prayers for themselves and
all who still remain. Thus at every great turn of
our lives, the church of stone reads us a lesson about
the Church of human spirits, and reminds us that we
are indeed members one of another.

I have left myself but little time to speak about
baptism, but all that has been now said about the
Church is a help towards understanding baptism
likewise. There are several lights in which baptism
may be truly regarded, but one of the most important, and I fear the oftenest forgotten, is that to which
we are led by the text and the doctrine which we
have been considering to-day. Next Sunday afternoon I hope to say to you more about the same
subject, and about confirmation, adding a few words
on the Church of England and Dissent. For the
present, let us think of baptism chiefly as the
entrance into the Church of Christ, the Holy Catholic
Church of which we speak in the creeds. Those
only will think this a poor and formal idea of
baptism who have themselves a poor and formal
idea of the Church. When a child is brought to
that font, it is brought in the presence of the whole
congregation in the midst of our weekly worship.
Not the clergyman alone, not the parents and sponsors alone are partakers in the solemn act. The
whole church acting through the clergyman receives
the child in the manner which Christ Himself com-

manded. The whole church gives thanks unto Almighty God for these benefits, and with one accord makes its prayers unto Him that the child may lead the rest of his life according to this beginning. And of those benefits for which the congregation gives thanks, one is that the child is grafted into the body of Christ's Church. The child is not left alone to fight its way through a rough and troublesome world. It is acknowledged as a child of the Christian family. All Christian people are declared to be its brothers and sisters. It has henceforth a right to look for Christian help and sympathy and love from one and all, since all are members of one body, and the greatest cannot say to the least, " I have no need of thee." As it grows up to manhood, it takes its place among the worshippers as one whose hope is in Christ. This and much more than this baptism gives to those who are brought by it into Christ's Church. Brethren, if this seems to you a fancy picture, if you cannot recognize these blessings in those who have been baptized here, let us—you and me—ask ourselves whether it may not be we that have made the grace of God of none effect.

VIII

BAPTISM AND CONFIRMATION

St. Ippolyts, Third Sunday after Epiphany, 1867.

" As ye have therefore received Christ Jesus the Lord, so walk ye in him; rooted and built up in him, and stablished in the faith as ye have been taught, abounding therein with thanksgiving."—*Col.* ii. 6, 7.

I BEGAN last Sunday afternoon to speak to you on the subject of the confirmation which, as you have heard, will be held in less than two months from this time. You will remember that I pointed out how impossible it is to understand confirmation while we are ignorant about baptism, and how impossible to understand baptism unless we know and believe in the Church into which we enter by baptism. That therefore was the subject which chiefly occupied us last Sunday, the Church ; not the building called a church in which we are now met, not even the Church of England, that body to which we belong and Dissenters do not, but the Church of Christ, the Holy Catholic Church, in which we declare that we all believe every time that we repeat the creeds. Of course I did not attempt to bring before you all that

might be truly said about the Church, but only so
much as it most concerns you to know for the right
understanding of baptism and confirmation.   Let me
repeat once more in a few words the chief matter of
the sermon.

The Church is the whole number of Christian
people who ever lived at any time, and who are
now living in any place.   Every one of us equally
has the high honour and blessing of being a member
of that great body, joined to Christ Himself, and
called *His* body, filled with the one Holy Spirit
from whom all draw their life.   We too here have
in this parish a part of that great universal Church,
a part through which we may enjoy the benefits
of the whole.   St. Paul speaks to us as to others:
he bids *us* remember that we are all knit together as
one in Christ ; he calls upon *us* not to live for ourselves, but for each other, to think of others, and
care for others, and be patient with others in all that
we think and say and do, because we all worship one
Lord, believe one faith, and begin our Christian life
from one baptism.

What is our ordinary practice?   How do these
commands of St. Paul agree with our every-day life?
Most of us care more or less for those of our own
family, and would make some sacrifices for their
sake.   Many of us have chosen friends of our own,
for whom in like manner we are at times willing
to do much.   And this, I fear, is nearly all.   St.
Paul's doctrine of the Church tells us on the other
hand that *all* members of the congregation make up
one family ; that none stand outside its circle, but all

have a right to our kindly feeling and our help. Even in our religion we are far too much each one for himself. The Lord's prayer teaches us to pray to *our* Father, to pray each as one of a company standing before God, all needing alike His forgiveness and His blessing, all eager to obtain for their neighbours whatever gift they desire for themselves. But what can we know about common prayers and mutual help in our religion, if our daily doings are selfish and suspicious and spiteful?

But if we wish to think of our brother Christians in our prayers, and to feel for them and act for them in our lives, we need the help of meeting together every week as Christians. Our church services have therefore a power which nothing else can supply, to keep before our minds that we are indeed members of one body, because we have one Head, even Christ. And so the outward church, the mere building of stones and mortar, holds together and supports the true living Church, which is the congregation. Here week by week we praise God together, and ask for His grace in our common needs ; here month by month we profess to meet to receive together the signs of Christ's love around His holy table. Here we welcome among us new members by baptism, and join our prayers and praises over the bodies of departed members before we commit them to the ground in the one common resting-place of our little congregation.

These thoughts about the Church have now brought us where we can begin to understand some part of the meaning of baptism. The first thing to notice about baptism is that it is the way of becoming a member of the Church. There is more in baptism than this ; but let us begin with this. I am afraid the common notion about baptism is that it is a curious ceremony which the clergyman performs upon an infant: that it usually takes place in church during service, but might just as well take place at any other time and even in any other place : that the congregation are only lookers-on, who interrupt their own prayers while the baptism is proceeding, and then go on with them again. This, I say, is certainly a common notion, yet an entirely wrong one. It is true that baptisms sometimes take place privately, when the child is likely to die before it can be safely brought to church : but that is because it is better that it should be baptized with only two or three present than not be baptized at all. It is true also that in some churches baptisms do not take place during service ; but that is a bad practice, not only because it prevents many of the congregation from ever taking part in a baptism, but because it confuses the minds of both parents and congregation as to what baptism really is. Here at least, where for many years baptisms have been performed during service, there ought to be no misunderstanding about the meaning of this arrangement.

The meaning is this. Baptism is the act not of the clergyman only, but of the whole congregation or Church. He speaks and acts in their name, because they are too many to speak and act for themselves. If you will carefully read the service, you will see how great a part they are meant to take in it. They

are no more lookers-on here than at any other part
of the common Sunday service. The clergyman is
no doubt the minister of God as well as the minister
of the people. But both duties are mixed together
here as at other times. Not in his own name, but in
the name of the people, does he say, "*We* receive
this child into the congregation of Christ's flock."
Before the actual baptism he calls on *all present*
to join together in prayers for the child : after the
actual baptism he calls on *all present* to join together
in praises for the benefits just received, and in fresh
prayers that the child may lead the rest of its life
according to this beginning.

   " We receive this child into the congregation of
Christ's flock."   These are the important words.
They tell us half the truth about baptism ; that
half which joins it on to what we have been learning
about the Church, and which points out to us the
chief interest that we all have in every baptism. We
are a congregation of Christ's flock. We stand here
in place of the great congregation of Christ's flock,
the Holy Church throughout the world. When a
child is brought to us by its parents and sponsors, we
receive it gladly, we welcome it, we offer a solemn
service to God in taking it among our number. In
so doing we remind ourselves that we are not a stray
set of people who have come together each for his own
convenience, each to say his own separate prayers;
but that we are one company, bound together by
common needs, a common salvation, and a common
belief in one Redeemer and Lord. The taking in of
a new member is therefore a warning to us to prize our

own membership more highly, and to keep constantly
in mind the sacred duties which we owe to the other
members.   Thus much for ourselves : and what are
we doing for the child by taking it among us, sinful
and careless as we are ?   Not, alas ! so much as we
might do for it, yet still much.   We take it from the
outer darkness and loneliness of the stormy world :
we treat it as from its earliest youth a Christian, one
whose true home is in the Church, who can rightly
look on its neighbours as friends and helpers, not as
rivals and enemies.   As it grows up, all Christian
influences are around it, not by accident, as might
happen to a child not baptized, but as its proper
right.   It has not to win its way by special trials so
as to be counted as one of the worshippers of Christ.
That is its proper place already : none can say to it
"I have no need of thee."

'And so the years pass by, and at last the child has
grown up to youth, and is of age to be confirmed.   It
was accepted as a Christian by its baptism in infancy,
though it was too young to know or understand anything about Christ, much less believe in Him.   Yet
the Church is made up of Christian people, that is of
those who do confess Christ ; and therefore it is but
right that the same profession should be openly made
by those who were too young to make it for themselves before.   This too takes place before the
Church, not merely before the little congregation
who joined in the baptism, but before a larger
Church made up of several congregations.   And
it is no longer an ordinary clergyman who performs
the service, but the bishop.   He being set over the

congregations in a large extent of country, his presence and office remind us of the great Catholic Church of which we are members, and teach us to think of the other congregations besides our own who are ever worshipping the same Lord, and towards whom it is right that we should cherish a true brotherly feeling.

Let us now turn to the other part of baptism, which also will presently lead us on to another view of confirmation.

Thus far we have considered baptism as the entrance into the Church. That is in the strictest sense a religious blessing, one which brings us near to God as well as to our brother men; for as members of the Church we are united to Christ through them, as well as united to them through Christ. Now we have to consider how baptism is the act of God and God alone. This is a more difficult subject, and one in which we are very liable to fall into mistaken notions. But it is far too important to pass over, and it bears strongly on our ordinary lives. By baptism God declares us to be His children. Our first birth by which we come into the world is like that of other creatures. If we were to take our thoughts of ourselves from that, we should have to call ourselves only a higher kind of animals. God has taught us otherwise. By sending from heaven His blessed Son to take our nature, He has bidden us believe that we have more to do with Him than with any lower creature, He has taught us to say " Our Father," and to believe that we are indeed His children. This glorious message is declared to us all in the Bible, and repeated in different ways all through the Prayer Book. But He has further ordained a certain pledge by which each man may assure himself that he has a right to say, "I am a child of God"; and that pledge is baptism. Baptism is not a conjuring trick by which something starts into being within the child which was not there before. The water can do no more than common water. The words can do no more than common words. But the whole baptism, water and words together, is what Christ Himself appointed as the way of entrance into the kingdom of God. God by it formally acknowledges the child as His own, gives him by it a right and title to enter on all the benefits which belong to His children. Henceforth the child, as he grows up, may look back to his baptism, and take comfort from it in knowing that he is no stranger to the Almighty Lord in heaven above. Henceforth he may safely call that awful Being his Father, may come to Him without fear as a child comes to its earthly father, may believe that He is a forgiving Father, who owes his children no grudge for their offences against Himself, and, when He punishes them, punishes in love, that they may become more like Himself.

This, believe me, brethren, is no empty benefit. Those who will not trust the assurance which God gave them in their baptism are obliged to think that they can make themselves His children by some efforts of their own. They dare not call themselves by that happy name till they find in themselves a certain measure of faith, or certain changes of feeling, about which it is most easy to be deceived. Some grow troubled and restless, because they dare not trust their own feelings as having reached what they suppose to be the necessary point, and indeed know them to be fickle and weak, and so cannot tell whether they have a Father in heaven or no. Others are very confident indeed that they are themselves children of God; but as they are equally confident that most of their neighbours are not, their belief fills them with spiritual pride, and a humble and child-like spirit is the very last that we can expect to find in them. And others again who are disposed to lead a careless life, yet are full of good impulses, are apt to go altogether astray just because they want the help and encouragement of knowing that God is *their* God already, and that He is willing and ready to support them with His grace in every effort that they make to do His will. From all these evils we may, if we please, be delivered by relying on the assurance of our baptism. To trust to the mere baptism itself, as if it had any power of its own, would be a dangerous folly. But to trust the promises of God, as brought home to ourselves by His holy baptism, is for most of us the highest wisdom.

This setting forth of God as our Father, of a new birth within us, a birth from above, a birth of the Spirit, that is, of our having an inner life which gives us power to hold communion with Him, is free and without condition. But what can it profit us if we act as if it were all false? Of what use to us are these great blessings if we do nothing but disobey

God's holy will, and grieve His Spirit, and live a
selfish animal life without one thought of Him?
His gifts are unprofitable to us, if we are unable or
unwilling to use them.   It is right therefore that
those who accept His gifts should declare their faith
in Him, and their desire to do His will.   Now this
is impossible for new-born infants.   They cannot
declare their own acceptance of their position as His
children, and yet it would not in general be well that
they should be received into the Church without a
word being said about the faith and obedience which
they will owe to Him as soon as their hearts and
minds are open to receive any knowledge of Him.
And so the promise is made for them by those who
bring them to the font.   It is a strange and mon-
strous error to fancy that the godfathers and godmothers carry the weight of the children's sins before
God till confirmation, and then shift them to the
children's shoulders from off their own.   This notion
is against all God's dealings with men.   The godfathers and godmothers, by promising on their behalf
do declare that they mean and wish them to be
true Christian children, Christ's faithful soldiers and
servants.   They also charge themselves with the
duty of either bringing them up in a Christian way,
or seeing that others do it.   They are not to be
held guilty of the children's sins except so far as
these are caused by their carelessness and neglect.
In that, no doubt, they have usually grievous reason
to condemn themselves.   And so the children must
bear their own burden, whether they be confirmed or
no.   Be their parents or sponsors ever so careful

and anxious, they will often break loose themselves, and choose to live as though they were the devil's children. And when they do this, they cannot plead that their sponsors will have to answer for it, for the sin is their own.

But, though confirmation has no power to shift to the children any guilt which they would not have to bear just the same without confirmation, it does mark the time when they depend more on themselves than they have done in former years. They have reached an age when they can understand the promises made in their name so many years before, and so it is right that they should say Amen in their own name. This is *their* part in being confirmed, to complete their baptism by welcoming it and accepting it and saying Amen, 'so be it,' to all which it says for them. By this they declare their wish to live as God's children, and as members of Christ's body the Church. New thoughts and new feelings are opening to them with the natural course of their growth. They have found out how hard it is to stand alone in the right way. Yet they do long to stand and not to fall, and so they throw themselves on the support of the Father who made them, the Son who redeemed them, and the Holy Spirit who makes them holy, and they desire also to be sustained by their brother Christians around them who are striving towards the same end. This they do, and God meets them. Once more His hand is stretched out to bless them. In confirmation His help is given to confirm and strengthen them in the new life on which they are entering, and He assures

them that He has not ceased to be their Father for
all their past disobedience, but is longing to cheer
them onward on their heavenward road.

Such, brethren, is the meaning of confirmation.
It is a help towards leading a right and Christian
life; a carrying on of that first great help which
baptism gives, by bringing before us at once our
powerlessness to do any good thing without God's aid,
and His willingness to aid and save us to the uttermost, seeing that we are His dear children; a carrying on likewise of the help which baptism gives, by
showing us that we are members of a goodly company of which Christ· is the Head, and leading us
to support each other with mutual encouragement.
There are some who are always ready to cry down
confirmation as a mere form. How that can be a
mere form which makes us feel that without God we
can do nothing, I cannot imagine. If I believed
that confirmation led young people to trust to the
effects of a single service performed upon them on a
single day, rather than to lean on their Saviour and
their God for every day of their future lives, I would
not for the world ask any one to be confirmed. If
the thing is good, if it brings heaven nearer to earth,
and gives strength where strength is sorely needed,
we need not trouble ourselves with foolish objections,
but thankfully use the means placed within our
reach.

I do not wish however to conceal that there is
another side to confirmation. It is not only a
renewal of the early promise to believe in God and
Christ, and to yield the willing obedience of chil-

dren; nor is it only the receiving of a fresh assurance
of strength and support from the Father who never
forsakes the work of His own hands.   It is also a
sign of a resolution to belong to the Church of
England.   On this too I must say a few words,
though they can be only few to-day.   I cannot at
the end of a sermon attempt to discuss at full length
the reasons why we ought to be Churchmen and not
Dissenters.   But it would not be right to pass the
subject over in total silence.   To those who join
Dissenting congregations, because they seriously and
calmly object to what they find in the Church of
England, I shall not now say anything.   There are
probably very few such among us.   Most of those
who follow Dissent, or are half inclined to follow it,
do so for no strong or well considered reason, but
for mere love of change or other such fancy, and
sometimes even for mere convenience or outward
advantage.   I would ask all such to think over what
I have said about the blessing of believing that we
are all members of one body, pledged to comfort
and support each other; and to consider how wantonly and mischievously we throw away the blessing
by separating ourselves from the church of this
parish for some trifling or unworthy reason.   The
loss is not only to ourselves but to others.   The
more we hold together with one hearty strong spirit,
the more surely does the power of Christ rest upon
us, and the more we can rely on each other's good
will and succour in the things of heaven or the
things of earth.   There is no such ground of Christian fellowship as a regular steady habit of worship-

ping in church together. If we go idly wandering about to this or that place, we do but breed a feebleness and lukewarmness of spirit which soon leaves us and our neighbours a prey to all the passions and jealousies which are ever ready to divide us from each other and so from our Father in heaven. I am very far from saying that none but those who hold fast to the Church of England have any right to call themselves members of the Church of Christ. But I do say most earnestly that many of the best blessings meant for the Church of Christ are lost by those who wander away from the Church of England.

For every reason therefore confirmation is a thing to be desired by those who wish to live a Christian life. I cannot invite those who have no such wish: to them it would be a mockery. It comes with a message of quiet joy and peaceful strength to those who feel the path of duty cold and cheerless, yet know that if they leave it, they will be banishing themselves from their true home. " I am not alone, for the Father is with me." " I can do all things through Christ that strengtheneth me." " The Spirit itself helpeth our infirmities." These are some of the cheering words which it speaks to us in our distress. It tells also of the like trials undergone by our brethren around us, and of the new power which springs up through striving with them instead of against them. More than this, it tells us of the multitudes who have gone before, members of the same Church who have departed this life in God's faith and fear, and holds up to us their bright examples

to light us on our way. "Ye are come," says the
Epistle to the Hebrews, "to the city of the living
God, the heavenly Jerusalem, and to an innumerable
company of angels, to the general assembly and
Church of the first-born which are written in heaven,
and to God, the Judge of all, and to the spirits of
just men made perfect, and to Jesus the Mediator of
the new Covenant." In this presence, brethren, we
all stand, whether we know it or not. These are
looking down on us now and always. Shall we
cause them to turn away their eyes in grief at our
careless and ungodly ways, or shall we look up and
welcome their gladdening presence to guide us and
support us to the land of peace?

IX

THE DISCOVERY AND ACKNOWLEDGMENT OF SIN

Emmanuel College Chapel, First Sunday in Lent, 1885.

"IF we say that we have no sin, we deceive ourselves, and the truth is not in us. If we confess our sins, he is faithful and righteous to forgive us our sins, and to cleanse us from all unrighteousness. If we say that we have not sinned, we make him a liar, and his word is not in us."— 1 *John* i. 8-10.

WAS there any need, we are tempted to think, for St. John to use this strong language? Can any one be found proud or foolish enough to assert what St. John denies, to say calmly he has no sin? Yes, St. John's words strike not at one here and another there among us, but at all. It is because of an almost universal doubt as to the reality of sin that his words are so fitted to be spoken to every Christian congregation at the beginning of their worship. It is not too much to speak thus of "our" doubt, though not many will at once recognize this state as their own. Described thus broadly, the notion is shocking to ordinary Christians. How can it be supposed, they ask, that we believe there is no such thing as sin, when we hold the Bible in our hands, and come to church, and join without repugnance in the prayers which everywhere imply its existence? Surely, they would say, such doctrines of unbelief, when not arising from reckless immorality, are confined to a few specu- lative dreamers who bewilder themselves with their own subtleties till they are lost out of the circle of Christian truth. We may not approve, they will perhaps go on, the violent and incessant harping upon sin which is heard so frequently from pulpits : it is but natural perhaps that those whose business it is to teach religion should deepen the shadows in their pictures of our lives, and strive to rouse their hearers by an excessive seriousness of tone : we take leave to form a more moderate and rational view about sin, but as for denying its existence, we are not such infidels as that.

There is truth as well as honesty in such a protest. A clear and conscious denial of sin is not often found separate from a disbelief in Christian truth at large. Yet a latent doubt about sin, or to say the least, a very feeble apprehension of its reality is well-nigh universal.

But what are the influences which produce this doubt, making us all less sensitive to sin than the Christians of other days? As usual, various in- fluences are combined. One of the strongest is connected with a sense of justice which we may fairly claim as distinctive of our own time, if not of ourselves. We see the evil there is in good men, and the good there is in evil men, with a readiness un- known before. This is a gain. But it is not a gain to be led to look at mankind as all alike, bathed in a grey twilight in which the different shades are as nothing beside the general likeness of tint, and in which neither light nor darkness seem to have any place. Again, it is well to recognize the great variety of circumstances which go to the building up of character, to confess how difficult it is for us to judge any man when we can know so little how much of his average disposition, how much in any one of his acts is of his own making, and how much has been made for him by the pressure of things without. But it is not well to forget that the choice between good and evil is ever lying before him, and that, though we may not judge him, there is One who can track out the evil and the good to the uttermost, One therefore who can judge him, and who will. These are the criticisms we pass upon others. But are we not ready to allow them to be applied to us, nay, to direct them upon ourselves? Yes, many of us are well content to do this ; but what does it amount to? We spread our own life out before us as a picture, a dead thing outside of us. We amuse ourselves with studying it in different lights and at different distances, now with our ordinary eyesight, now as through a telescope, now as through a microscope. We observe the evil as well as the good just as we should do in studying the life of others. But what do we mean by the evil and the good? Is not our recognizing the evil beside the good in ourselves too often like recognizing the blue beside the red? We see that they are different : we are interested to watch the play of one within the other with hardly more than a faint regret when evil prevails. We forget that the one means life and the other means death.

This is one of our moods. At times our self-criticism has less in it of a deadly calm. Those two words, good and evil, expand with a fresher power. We feel evil not merely as a colour in a picture, not merely as a quality to be regretted, but as an enemy to be striven against. Yet for the most part we condemn it chiefly either as folly, or as unkindness. Looking back on our past experience, we cannot but see how often we have deeply, nay, irreparably injured ourselves ; how often we have acted and are acting still in perverse blindness to our own welfare. This is one of the forms of evil which we quickly discern. The other has reference to other people, our relations, our friends, our habitual or casual neighbours. Our conscience smites us for much in our behaviour towards them, the kindnesses we might have rendered them and have not, the positive wrongs we have done them through selfishness, or even through jealousy and spite. We may not be able to explain to ourselves why we should trouble ourselves about them at all, but we know that, when we greatly disregard them, the world goes out of joint with us, and there is a jar which is not pleasant to bear. It is well to strive against our own folly and our own unkindness, but for most men it will be a feeble struggle if they are not nerved by a mightier spirit within them, even the hatred of sin ; and that they cannot have while sin is to them only a familiar term of theology. Evil towards ourselves,

evil towards others, is but half known in its evilness
till it is known in the light of God.   Here we touch
the last and most potent cause of our faint apprehension of sin.   We have but a weak hold on God: how
then can our belief in the reality of sin be vigorous
enough to deserve the name?.   If we push our
questions further, and ask why God presents so
faint an image in these days even to those who
are really and truly devoted to His service, we enter
on a subject too wide to deal with directly to-day.
We‧ must return to our immediate subject.

Sometimes it is boldly said, ‘ More than enough
has been talked about evil, and especially about sin,
in the past ages of Christendom ; and not much
good has come of it.   Better far let the dead bury
their dead.   Better leave Lents, and calls to repentance, and lamentations for sin, to perish with the
dark times which gave them birth.   Better trust
wholly for the future to a bright and cheerful
religion, and try whether sunshine cannot prevail
where the thundercloud has failed.’   This is very
tempting advice.   No doubt the Christian faith has
never yet completely unfolded its character as first
and last a gospel.   We have been grovelling far too
long in Christ's tomb, and forgetting that He is
risen.   We have distrusted the healing power of
hope and joy.   This is not only true, but a truth
which is never out of season.   We cannot keep a
Christian Lent if we forget for a moment that it
ends in an Easter.   Yet nevertheless we dare not
give up our Lent, and its unwelcome memorial of
sin; because, if we do, we take a step backward

indeed, we return once more into the world as it was
before Christ came, with its miserable alternatives of
a delirious gaiety, which vainly strove by reckless
indulgence to forget its own hollowness and hopeless-
ness, and of the abject despair of those who, through
fear of death, were all their lifetime subject to bondage.
Till we sink deep enough into ourselves to know sin
in all its bitterness with a knowledge which makes all
ordinary belief seem shadowy and dim, we have no
access to the perennial fountain of light and glory,
we must content ourselves with such poor gleams
of light and glory as pass over us and then vanish
away.

Already in the days of St. John there were
Christians for whom the word ' sin ' was beginning
to lose its meaning. We greatly mistake the text if
we suppose it merely to pronounce one of the
commonplaces of religion for the benefit of ordinary
readers, who were in danger only from moral indifference. It is aimed at a positive doctrine, one
more distinct than any of the same character widely
spread among us, and arising, for the most part, from
different causes, yet in result not unlike our own
manner of thinking. It is very instructive to observe
how St. John is led to speak of sin. The coming of
Christ in the flesh and the new knowledge of God,
which had dawned upon man through His coming,
are the subjects which fill his mind from the
beginning of the Epistle to the end. "We know that
the Son of God is come, and hath given us an understanding that we may know him that is true, and we
are in him that is true, as being in his Son Jesus

Christ ": these, almost the closing words, might serve as a text to the whole. The opening verses have the same meaning in ampler and yet more pregnant language. St. John's own personal converse with the Master, on whose breast he had leaned, was to himself a revelation of the life which is in God, and which from Him flows forth to men: and this knowledge of his he imparted to a younger generation of Christians, that they also might be joined in the fellowship of life with the Father and the Son into which it had brought himself, so that their common joy might be complete. Life, fellowship, joy, these are the leading words from which he starts. If he afterwards descends to a lower level, it is for fear these priceless treasures should be lost unawares.

Taking his stand on this foundation he strikes at once at one of the plausible falsehoods with which his disciples were beguiling themselves. It would seem that they thought it must be unworthy of God to vex Himself about the right or wrong doings of men ; they pictured Him as so great and comprehensive that He contained within Himself darkness as well as light, and looked with equal complacency on the evil and the good, so that what men call wrongdoing was not sin against Him, and therefore on a large view of creation deserved no condemnation. St. John knew that such a being had nothing in common with the Father of his Lord Jesus Christ, who had suffered and died to put away the sins of the world. On the strength of his fellowship with the very life of God, which had made itself known in his own spirit through the person of Jesus, he declares that God is light without any mixture of darkness, and that men can be partakers of His life only by refusing to do the works of darkness.

Then, it might be pleaded, he said, fellowship between men and God is impossible till men are sinless, for there is always darkness mixed with their light. Nay, he replies, those spots of darkness on the human spirit are not indelible: the blood of God's own Son has power to wash them out. We may, we must, find it hard to picture ourselves the manner in which he supposed this mystic washing to be brought about. But there is no doubt as to his general meaning. In the heavenly virtue of Christ's sacrifice, he would say, lies the only possible abolition of sin. Do not dream of any other, he goes on in the text : do not hope to juggle away sin by pretending there is no such thing : corruption does not lose its ugliness by giving it a fair name. Perhaps you think you have cleared away a great difficulty out of the path of mankind and opened out the way to a new and brighter ideal of life. But this is the rankest self-deception : you are but kindling a torch of crazy theory, and wilfully shutting out the light of truth which enters those who hold personal converse with the life of God. Nay, the way to life lies in exactly the opposite direction. It is not enough to refuse to say that we have no sin. We must press forward to confess our sins, to carry them with shame before God for Him to abolish. And that He will surely do both towards Himself and towards us. As sins in the proper sense of the word, offences against a loving Father and Maker, He will send them away, forgive

them, allow them to make no breach between Him
and us. As unrighteousnesses, as stains and injuries
to our own natures which He created for righteousness, He will cleanse them away and enable us to go
forth in newness of life. Let us have no fears about
His will to do this : it rests upon His very faithfulness
and righteousness : in doing it He is not indulgently
breaking in upon the strict law of His nature, but
acting as His external nature requires Him to act ;
He is but perfecting what He began, refusing to
despise the work of His own hands, carrying out the
purpose for which He sent His Son to die. And if,
once more, in spite of the revelation of God as the
destroyer of sin, we say that for our part we have
committed no sin, we do more than deceive ourselves,
more than refuse to receive the truth within us, we
set ourselves directly against God in person, making
Him a liar, smothering His voice within us.

Such is, I think, the meaning of the text; and
now, it may be asked, how does it meet the state of
mind in ourselves which makes us indifferent and
half-incredulous about sin ? Only by the revelation
which it makes of the nature of God and the work
of God; on the one hand, His absolute purity and
separateness from sin, His undying hostility to sin;
on the other, His perfect willingness to abolish sin
and the memory of sin. The text has no other
kind of argument. Argument can never convince a
man that he has sinned, and unless he has known
what sin means in himself he will misunderstand it
in others. The bitter sense of having been guilty of
rebellion and ingratitude and coldness against the

God of his life is not a thing that can be created by
any process of the understanding. The work of
argument can be only destructive, to clear away the
false reasoning by which we persuade ourselves that
the sense of sin *must* be a delusion. But so far as
our perverse thoughts are suggested or encouraged
by the prevalence of unworthy or imperfect views of
Christ's coming, so far the text may render us great
service by teaching us better things. In the gospel
sin and the forgiveness of sin are always coupled
together. Before the gospel the sense of sin was
either a nullity or an unbearable torment. How
great was its power to madden a sensitive conscience
we may read in the early chapters of the Epistle to
the Romans, and St. Paul's experience has been
shared in after ages by many an ill-taught Christian.
Can we seriously believe that St. Paul would have
become either a better or a happier man if he could
have persuaded himself that all his inward torments
arose from no corresponding reality? When at
length he grew into the peace which passeth all
understanding, his sense of sin was not less though
it changed its form, testifying no longer to a broken
law of dead ordinances, but to the wounded love of
a living God.

The power of the Christian faith, brethren, lies in
this, that it ignores no dark fact of human life, while
it proclaims deliverance from all. Without it we are
helpless to escape from one of two alternatives, unless
we drench ourselves in riotous living. Either we
must suffer the misery of helplessly watching the
apparent triumph of evil in those things which most

concern mankind, or we must wrap ourselves in a
thin and half-imaginary persuasion that evil is after
all only another kind of good. The Christian faith
fearlessly accepts the worst, and then points to God
in His Son victorious over every enemy of man. It
speaks not of life without death, but of life overcoming death. It confesses sin, and in the same
breath declares the forgiveness of sin. This is no
empty cancelling of both sides. The sinner who
knows that he is forgiven, and knows what forgiveness is, will never dream of that. Time was when
God was only known to him by the hearing of the
ear, and sin was only known to him by the hearing
of the ear. Then the true natures of both were
revealed to him together in one penetrating flash;
how can he ever be as though that had not been?
Experience shows that, if we think lightly of our past
misdoings, they retain their full power to cramp and
deprave our later life. Yet assuredly they were not
meant to haunt us as ghastly spectres of memory.
There is no way out of the contradiction but through
a firm belief in God's forgiveness—not His indifference, but His forgiveness, which has power to change
the substance of our darkest recollections by a
heavenly chemistry of its own, so that we are sent
forth upon our way sorrowful yet alway rejoicing.
Hard it is to believe in forgiveness in the truest
sense, perhaps harder to believe in it than in anything else that we are called on to believe in. But
the Word of God stands sure, " If we confess our
sins, He is faithful and righteous to forgive us our
sins, and to cleanse us from all unrighteousness."

X

SELF-RESTRAINT THE CONDITION OF MASTERY

Emmanuel College Chapel, Third Sunday in Lent, 1878.

" EVERY man that striveth for the mastery is temperate in all things. Now they do it to obtain a corruptible crown, but we an incorruptible."
—1 *Cor.* ix. 25.

THE wise book of Ecclesiastes says, "To every thing there is a season, and a time to every purpose under the heaven, a time to weep and a time to laugh, a time to mourn and a time to dance." Weeping and laughter, mourning and joy, are both alike parts of a reasonable and, in the best sense, natural life; and the Bible, speaking in its divine breadth to the whole nature of man, sanctions and hallows and elevates both alike. All common joy, all common sorrow, are in God's eyes right and good when they do not come from sinful causes. But in proportion to the worthiness of their occasions, and the guilelessness of heart with which we receive them, do they rise up to that highest joy and that highest sorrow which are born within us when we set before our minds God and Christ, and the whole breadth of His redeeming work, and our own standing before Him, our weakness, our sin, and our restoration to the heaven of filial communion with Him.

Now in Lent the darker side of our own life is brought forcibly before our minds. Neither now nor at any time, thank God, are we required or even allowed to forget the infinite grace shown in all God's dealings with us, the glory of the children of God. But for the time we move chiefly in shadow, though we do not forget the light beyond. The honest, unaffected sense of unworthiness and failure, which should not be wholly absent from our minds on any day of the year, ought now to lie upon us with a deeper and heavier stress, lest we lightly cast it away from us altogether, and shut our eyes for ever on God and His holy law.

But a self-reproachful sense of failure is of little use till it has been set to do work. In the text, taken along with its context, St. Paul tells us the work which he set his self-reproachful sense of failure to do. It was nothing less than the work of self-conquest, that deliberate restraint of mere impulses of all kinds, but especially of the impulses of the body, which is called temperance. He is speaking from his own experience, declaring what he found to be his own daily need. He was writing to men who were great sticklers for liberty. He was as resolute a champion of liberty as any man could be; he was never tired of denouncing those feeble Christians who allowed themselves to ascribe divine authority to earthly rules. But he knew well the poor, worthless hollownesses which we are all apt to take for liberty, and he wrote down plainly *his* way of making himself a free man. And that was by putting the strictest control on himself, by not making it his maxim to do what he liked. He was like other men in wishing to be free; he was unlike other men in what he believed freedom to be, and in the way that he went about to obtain freedom.

Unlike other men, and yet not altogether unlike some whom all agreed to respect after a certain manner. That is the drift of the text. St. Paul here declares that the Christian life is a higher and nobler copy of the life led by others not Christians, who were wise in what they did for their own particular object. When he said, " Every man that striveth for the mastery is temperate in all things," he had in view, as we all know, one particular kind of mastery, mastery in the games of strength and skill which were held in the neighbourhood of Corinth. Men who wanted to be thought Christians chafed at any restraint upon their appetites and wishes. They craved to go their own way, and that in the name of the gospel. " What!" he says, "Have you forgotten what pains the runners in a foot-race take to put themselves in a way to win the prize ? Have you not noticed how, if they are really in earnest about winning, they for a long while before the race abstain from strong drink and excess of food, and from every other luxury which might soften and weaken the power and activity of their bodies ? And do you expect to prevail in the Christian race, that race in which the meek and

crucified Jesus is the judge, if you are not willing
to give up your own rights or your own pleasures?"

This is the meaning of the first half of the text
expressed in other words. But I think we may at
this time fix the lesson more deeply in our hearts by
looking beyond the example which St. Paul had
chiefly in view. For his purpose it was enough to
put forcibly together the lowest and the highest
instances of temperance, the training for a race, and
the life which befits them whom Christ has redeemed.
But in truth there is no part of human life in which
this same truth is not entirely true, and greatly
needed. We mount to the height of an Apostle's
holy mind by a series of steps, each of which in its
own way repeats the universal law, "He that striveth
for the mastery is temperate in all things."

Let us examine a few of these steps, beginning, as
St. Paul did, at the lowest. The mastery sought by
the runner in a race has in it nothing that can
properly be called spiritual. Strength and supple-
ness of body are all at which he aims. These are
powers which no wise man despises, precious gifts of
God to those who possess them, meant to be used for
His service. But in themselves there is nothing
divine, nothing of that which marks out man from
the rest of the creatures. They are to be found in
the greatest perfection in animals, and are not even
the highest qualities which animals sometimes show.
Now we know well that, if we wish to increase our
strength and speed, we must, in St. Paul's words, "be
temperate in all things." It is only by a certain
amount of such temperance that we keep our bodies

in health at all. If we give ourselves up habitually without restraint to indulging any of their appetites, we sow the seeds of weakness and disease. And on the other hand, there is no way of bringing our bodily powers to greater perfection but by practising far more than our usual abstinence. Thus we cannot obtain the mastery even for the body itself except by stinting and keeping within bounds its own wild desires. Such temperance must certainly be called wise, but it does not always imply any kind of goodness. Even a wicked man may wish to be strong : we must know for what ends the strength is to be used before we can very greatly admire him who labours to obtain it. But his efforts still make up a wholesome example. In this, as in so many ways, the children of this age are in their generation wiser than the children of light.

Let us now pass on to another kind of mastery, what we may call the mastery of success in life. Here we are at once on human ground. Success in life means for the most part making our way prosperously among the men with whom we have to live, securing a certain portion of the means of subsistence, perhaps increasing it, or, it may be, acquiring power over others, or honour and respect from others. Once more, these are not things which call at once for praise : sometimes they deserve to be condemned as the pursuits of an earthly and selfish mind ; they are always contemptible when they take the *first* place in a man's thoughts. But of those who gain no such success, who fail in whatever they attempt, we naturally and even rightly say that there is some

H

flaw or defect in their character. God forbid that
we should say this of such as often seem to men to
lack success because their portion is always poverty
or contempt, only through the utter heavenliness and
unworldliness of their lives. They do not fail ;
they succeed in their own pursuits ; what they seek,
they do find. But in their case and in that of those
whom all men see to be successful, the same rule
stands true. " He that striveth for the mastery is
temperate in all things." If we study their characters
as they now lie open before us ; if we trace, as far as
we are able, their course from boyhood till now in all
the little as well as the great affairs of daily life, we
invariably find this one feature stamped on their
conduct, they were temperate in all things. They
have been able to command their fellowmen, to
command the hard and grinding world, because they
first learnt to command themselves, to command
themselves in the fullest sense of the words, that is,
to command all that was within them.

The first and most necessary lesson was to command their bodies. Whoever has not learned that
is a helpless slave, wasting on short-lived and utterly
fruitless pleasure, time, money, health—everything
necessary for any kind of success ; always liable to
have the work of laborious years undone by a brief
space of worthless enjoyment. But self-command
includes more than command of the body. The
mind too has its own desires, above all its desires
of what it takes for freedom. These too we shall
always find have been kept under with a strong hand
by those who have attained any great measure of

success. We are apt to think that success consists in having our own way. On the contrary, all such men have gained their ends by forcing themselves, not once or twice, but habitually, to do without having their own way, and especially by resisting all those random impulses of the moment which increase wonderfully upon those who once yield to them. For indeed most of our fancied freedom is an idle dream. All through life we are hemmed in at every turn by a thousand powers of which we take no heed, till we have run against them unawares to our own harm. True freedom, such freedom as we *can* enjoy, begins when we have learned to conquer our unruly selves, and so to place ourselves that the laws of God may be on our side, and not against us. This is indeed being temperate in all things, not hurting or destroying any good thing which God has given us, but so restraining all our wishes and desires that they never can, as it were, run away with us. And this, once more, is the one sure means of mastery in the affairs of life. He that thinks first of enjoying himself or pleasing himself is thereby stamped for ever as hopelessly helpless and weak. He that keeps himself under and is always temperate has learned the secret of human greatness ; by such, and such alone, the world is subdued to their use.

Again, there is a mastery of a far nobler sort, always and under all circumstances worthy of admiration, the mastery of enforcing justice and right. There is in all of us, very faint, it is to be feared, in some, yet not wholly wanting in any, a desire to do only what is right, and that everyone may have what is justly their due. We feel indignant at anything like unfairness and foul play. We long to see all crooked things made straight. We are willing to put up with loss or pain ourselves rather than be guilty of injustice. But to act on these right and worthy feelings requires a steady strength of character; and that is nowhere to be found where there is not first temperance in all things.

But perhaps we may say to ourselves that, though justice and right require the calm and steady mind of temperance, our affections do not. We may fancy that our love for each other may glow with the utmost fervour, though we be unable to practise any self-control. Perhaps we may cherish a secret belief, that temperance is rather a cold and lifeless thing, and that they are likely to have the warmest hearts who give the fullest play to every movement within. A woeful delusion, which has been the ruin of thousands. It may perhaps be true, that the evil which the want of temperance works in the soul will spare our affections longest. But assuredly they are enemies to each other, not friends. All true affection requires a true and constant giving up of self, and therefore can suffer nothing but loss from the random passions of self. It is not fitful and capricious, blazing up violently for a little while and then burning itself rapidly out into cold darkness. It lives by the steady and often repeated efforts of self-restraint. For temperance has in itself nothing of a chilling or a deadening nature, though it may come easiest to persons of a cold and over sober temper. In reality, it keeps alive the strength of whatever is strong within us, sustaining it and feeding it by holding it within bounds. Thus here too the rule holds good. They that are made perfect in their affections, they who strive for and gain the mastery in warmth of heart, are they who are temperate in all things.

We have now gone through different steps of human nature, in all of which we have found the mastery given by self-control: strength of body, success in life, power to do justice and right, strength and lastingness of affection, all are denied to him who does not always strive to be temperate in all things: and all these things are good, though not the highest good. Surely we cannot doubt that the same universal law rules over us in the greatest height to which man can reach, in what we call religion, the love and service which refuse to stop short of God and His Son Jesus Christ. So at least St. Paul taught, and so he found in his own heart and life. " I therefore," he says, " so run, not as uncertainly: so fight I, not as one that beateth the air: but I keep under my body and bring it into subjection, lest that by any means, when I have preached to others, I myself should be a castaway." These are surely awful words to us, if we understand them. Let us only think of St. Paul; think of his wonderful conversion, think of the toils and sufferings which he underwent for the gospel's sake, the love of Christ which he felt constraining him, the love to God and man which impelled him ever onwards, the triumphant faith which carried him through; if ever a man was in the truest and best sense Christian, surely he was: and then let us remember that he had need to be temperate in all things, lest he should himself become a castaway.

In a lazy way, we are ready to admit that a Christian ought not to give the rein to his disorderly wishes and desires. But how little we mean what we say! How often those who pride themselves on their own spirituality and Christian experience give themselves up without scruple to self-indulgence so long as they do not outrage the common laws of morality! How rarely do those who know they are not living a Christian life, who wish to be Christians, but complain that they fail every time they try, take the first and most necessary step to even the lowest kind of mastery, the first lesson of self-restraint! Not one of us, assuredly, has in this matter a right to accuse another. Our only safe and right feeling is St. Paul's, a taking heed by every one who thinketh he standeth lest after all he fall. And if we are oppressed by our own miserable weakness, if we find out, as assuredly we must, that *in* ourselves *of* ourselves dwelleth no good thing, yet this too was St. Paul's experience. When he was weak, then it was he found himself strong, for then the power of Christ rested upon him, and Christ's strength was perfected in weakness. That we may share his experience both of evil and of good, God has given us this season. Let us then all begin now more earnestly than ever that steady effort to win self-control which more than anything else lays bare before us our own weakness: and then, falling on our knees before the heavenly throne, we shall find ourselves made strong in the Lord and in the power of His might.

XI

[REASONABLE SERVICE]¹

Ely Cathedral. Lent, 1875.

" I BESEECH you therefore, brethren, by the mercies of God, that ye
present your bodies a living sacrifice, holy, acceptable unto God, which
is your reasonable service.   And be not conformed to this world, but be
ye transformed by the renewing of your mind, that ye may prove what
is that good and acceptable and perfect will of God."—*Romans* xii. 1, 2.

WHAT St. Paul speaks to us here is no single or
partial lesson dropped by the way.   Standing where
it does in his writings, it carries an exceptional
weight of authority and breadth of meaning.   It
forms a kind of midpoint in the greatest and most
comprehensive of his early epistles.   If we are
desiring to know what he meant by Christian
doctrine, at least in its simpler elements, we turn
to the Epistle to the Romans.   The same epistle
is hardly less rich in instruction respecting his
view of Christian morality and practice, especially in
the wider relations of society at large.   The two
divisions of the epistle are joined together by our
text, itself St. Paul's own text and foundation for the

¹ This Sermon stands in the MS. without heading.

moral teaching which follows it, as it is at the same
time the immediate conclusion from the doctrinal
teaching which has gone before. As we read it,
we seem uplifted for the moment with him to
that height of true vision in which he beheld all
truth and all life as one.

The earlier chapters have had both a bright and a
dark side. The darkness is perhaps the more con-
spicuous : but it is preceded and penetrated and
surrounded by the light. At the head stands the
divine calling of the Apostle making appeal to the
divine calling of the Church of God's beloved, in the
name of the risen Son of God. Then the sad
experience of human failure in the past under
different forms is recounted ; but in each case out
of the fulness of the redemption in Christ Jesus
is drawn forth a special assurance of victory and
restoration, promised to the new power of faith.
Gentile and Jew alike have gone miserably to ruin in
the matter of righteousness : but God has provided
for both a new righteousness by faith in Him who
raised Jesus our Lord from the dead. Sin and death
reign in mankind, and no law of outward commandments has availed to do more than restrain in some
measure their outward activities : but God has freely
bestowed a new and eternal life in Christ Jesus our
Lord, and this life is a life of the Spirit, shrivelling up
sin from the very root. Thus the proved love of God
holds us fast to itself, though every power in the
universe should strive to tear us away : He who
sacrificed His own Son for our sakes must needs with
Him bestow on us all things. Nor is the perfectness

of the gift contradicted by the failure and rejection of God's own ancient people. In His counsels their fall has led to the entering in of the Gentiles on terms of mercy ; and even so shall they too be received back, not as of right but likewise of mercy : for God had shut up all into disobedience that He might have mercy upon all.

" I beseech you therefore, brethren," says St. Paul, " by the mercies of God." He is speaking to Jews and Gentiles alike, united in the one Church, all taught by their own several histories that a Christless world is a world on the way downwards into darkness and death, all now raised to a new and endless and fruitful life in the crucified and risen Lord, all receivers of this gift by no claim of wages earned but by the mercy of the God who loved them. This is the ground of St. Paul's present call to them. While the many lessons of the former eleven chapters, varying applications of the one Gospel, are still fresh in their minds,—before the awful hope called forth by the last doxology " From Him and through Him and unto Him are all things," has begun to die away,— he builds at once on these foundations a new exhortation, " I beseech you therefore." He speaks not to prudence or to fear. He assumes that the heavenly love has conquered them, and rules them still by its own pure sway.

He beseeches them by the mercies, the compassions, of God. Already in the Old Testament God's saints had loved to dwell on the multitude, the variety, the perseveringness, of God's compassions. St. Paul then does but take up the ancient strain,

while he is thinking chiefly of the new compassions
which made up the sum of his gospel. New compassions they were, yet not only new : they cast a
light back on all God's compassions in elder days, and
showed many acts of His to have been indeed compassions though hitherto they had lain only in gloom.
Yet still more did they shine forth into the future :
they were not merely undoings of past evil and its
consequences, but promises of a new life.

God's compassions in Christ had set God Himself
in the true light. This was their first and most
necessary work : so long as God's own purpose was
doubted or misunderstood, it was not possible to
render Him a rightful service. But His compassions
likewise set men in the true light. The many weary
efforts to dispense with God, or to deal with Him as
an equal, or if as a superior, then as a hard and
indifferent superior,—all those efforts had failed.
Till the experiment had been repeatedly tried, men
would not believe that they could not succeed: just as,
after so many more centuries of experience, many still
refuse to believe that they may not even now succeed.
But he who accepted the gospel laid all these dreams
at once aside. He stood only as one who had found
mercy. That was the starting point of all his
thoughts and ways. He was one who needed mercy,
and one who received it. If he was to do anything
aright, it must be through a sleepless sense that he
was a creature, an ever dependent creature, drawing
all his powers from above, all his best powers from
conscious recognition of Him who is above, free only
when obedient, often going astray and rebelling, yet

owing all his returns into the way of good to his slighted or rejected God. Such a mercy had in it nothing degrading to receive. It was not the contemptuous mercy wrung by bribes or entreaties from an indifferent or satiated despot, but the tenderest form of action assumed by a Father's spontaneous, vigilant, and manifold love. Forgiveness of past undutifulness was there, forgiveness that had been wrought out in a sacrifice which we can only dimly conceive. Without the forgiveness the mercy would have been no sure bond between the Giver and the receiver. But as the Only Son had been delivered up to death for our offences, in like manner He had been raised for our justification ; so that the mercy was even more a gift of power for the days to come than a gift of peace for the days gone by, and the peace of forgiveness itself became an ever renewed foundation for the peace of communion.

Thus then St. Paul has given expression to the chief thought that memory must ever carry to Christian men. The compassions of God are all about them. What fruit should His compassions bear, now that they are known through the gospel ? How should they shape the life which they have restored ? " I beseech you," St. Paul says, " to present your bodies a sacrifice, living, holy, well-pleasing to God." He speaks first here of the outward self, then in the next verse of the inward self. He calls for a sacrifice of our bodies. In the old time the bodies offered in sacrifice were those of bulls and goats, not men, but possessions of men. That order of sacrifice had now

passed away, since One had come who had borne
our sins in His own body to the fatal tree ; and in
His doing of the will of God we had been hallowed
by the offering of His body once for all. But sacrifice
itself had not therefore passed away from among mankind.   A riper and more complete form of sacrifice
had succeeded, no longer of our possessions only, but
of our very selves.   As Christ presented and offered
up His body for us, so must we, in the power of His
sacrifice, present our bodies. All must be yielded up
absolutely to the Father who made all and redeemed
all. We must not keep anything back for our own
control, much less for the independent control of the
body's own impulses.   But the sacrifices cease to be
Christian the moment they are looked upon as having
a virtue to prevail with God, winning His forgiveness
or His favour ; then they sink back to the lower
level of Jewish sacrifices now become futile.   The
riches of God's grace were poured out upon us in
Christ Jesus once for all ; day by day the Holy
Spirit supplies them to our daily need. The sacrifice
which St. Paul offered of his body in his unwearied
labours, and which he beseeches us all to offer of our
bodies, is a sacrifice of glad thanksgiving.

But it is a living sacrifice.   In this there is no
contradiction.   We sometimes fancy that sacrifice
must needs involve death, or at least suppression.
But it is not so.   True sacrifice involves that utter
offering of which death is the complete fulfilment.
But this sacrifice of the will is not always executed
in act.   The sacrifice of Abraham was a true sacrifice,
though Isaac was given back to him in life.   The

presenting, as St. Paul calls it, of Isaac was already complete ; faith had already done its work. " Let not sin reign in your mortal body that ye should obey the lusts thereof," says St. Paul in an earlier chapter. " Neither present ye your members as instruments of unrighteousness to sin, but present yourselves to God as alive from the dead, and your members as instruments of righteousness to God." Even so, when the desires of the body are recognized as having a title to obedience, or even when they are carelessly obeyed as a matter of fact, though their authority is in words denied, then sin is queen in our mortal body, and our members become ready instruments to do what sin commands. But when we present our very selves to God as a living sacrifice, alive with a new life, displacing the old sinful semblance of life which works only destruction, then by that same act we present our members to God as ready instruments of His righteousness. But this could not be if in sacrificing ourselves we always slew ourselves. The surrender of life to God is complete, but His will most commonly is to give us back the surrendered life as life from the dead. What fits us to work His righteousness is not death but life. The sins which seem to us in our blindness to be natural fruits of life are in truth the destroyers of life, the destroyers not only of spiritual but of bodily life, destroyers of the body's own noblest perfection. It is true that, when once we have set ourselves to resist the tyranny of natural desires, we are sorely tempted to picture God to ourselves as having pleasure in death. We neither trust His saving goodness enough,

nor enter into the largeness and variety of the uses
for which He asks His creatures' service. We accept
more readily the despairing heathen dream of a
crushed body than the Christian faith of a redeemed
body. But the apostolic doctrine remains strictly
true. The chastening and restraint by which we are
enabled to present our bodies as a sacrifice to God is
precisely that which makes them most alive.

But this living sacrifice must also be "holy." It
must be worthy of God's glory as well as fit for His
service, consecrated to One whose name is holy, set
apart from things base and vile. Reverence to God
will show itself in reverence to that which is hallowed
by His name. Sometimes we dishonour the body by
pampering it and making it our idol ; sometimes we
dishonour it by treating it with contemptuous neglect
and aversion. But God made it to be cherished with
reverence, though it is hard to understand what these
words mean till we have learned to present it as a
sacrifice to God, and that a living sacrifice. Un-
wavering rejection and abhorrence of all gluttony and
uncleanness is the foundation, but where this is
present, true reverence finds a grace and a good to
pursue as well as a foulness and an evil to flee. In
becoming holy to God, all things become capable of
being by right use themselves divine.

Once more the living, the holy sacrifice is to be
"well-pleasing to God." This condition embraces
both the others, but goes beyond them. All men
who ever offered sacrifice, unless it were in hypocrisy
or by mere custom, offered it as well-pleasing to the
god of their worship. But why they wished to please

their god was another matter ; their wish might come
from this or that of a whole range of paltry, or
indifferent, or lofty motives. Accordingly St. Paul,
knowing well the false thoughts of sacrifice which
spring up naturally in men's hearts, has left no room
for them in his exhortation. Against one false
thought of sacrifice he has set the need that it be
living ; against another he has provided by refusing
to recognize a sacrifice which, though living, is not
kept holy. But the universal thought of pleasing
God has a truth of its own which may not without
peril be forgotten. The livingness, the holiness are
in themselves well-pleasing to God, but it is possible,
strange and contradictory as it may seem, for men to
make the sacrifices, and to be careful about them in
both these respects, to speak much and act much on
the belief that sacrifice and life and holiness are truly
some great things, and yet to forget God Himself.
But when this happens, the whole meaning of sacrifice
is lost. " Thou shalt *love* the Lord thy God with all
thy heart and soul and strength" remains the first and
great commandment. The Christian desire of well-
pleasing has nothing to do with the hope of gain or
the fear of suffering, but is that desire of well-pleasing
which belongs to love and love alone. The supreme
value of sacrifice springs from the yearning of God's
children on earth for their Father in heaven.

This sacrifice then, thus presented, St. Paul tells us,
is the true form of divine service and worship for
Christians, their reasonable service, the service, that is,
which befits them as reasonable beings in all whose
acts reason is appointed to have a place. The old

divine service of the Levitical law, of which he has
spoken three chapters before, full as it was of meanings and purposes which reason could trace, was in
itself a mere performance of outward acts in which
there was no room for the exercise of reason. But
the new divine service of sacrifice embraced the whole
life. Every act was to be treated as part of a living,
holy, well-pleasing sacrifice. Unaided, the love of God
would suffice to inspire it and turn it into sacrifice,
but more it could not do. Other powers, powers
involving knowledge and wisdom, in a word, powers
of reason would be required to determine what
acts would be acts of *rightful* sacrifice and worship. Simple obedience to the precepts of the
ceremonial law or tradition had once been a sufficient
guide, but henceforth sacrifice was to be bound up
with the new and glorious responsibilities which
belong to knowledge.

And so we are led to the second verse, in which
St. Paul carries on his exhortation from the outer
self to the inner self. He has bidden us present our
bodies to God, and suggested high thoughts of their
dignity and capacity. But each word that has come
before us, and especially the last, has led us upward
towards the region of man's spiritual nature, for
there too he has a message to deliver on the strength
of the compassions of God. He begins with describing the true nature of that seductive web of motives
from which the acceptance of sacrifice is meant to
deliver us. "And be not conformed," he says, "to
this world," to the outward framework of this present
stage of existence. Do not take your shape from

things around you, for then you condemn yourself to sinking instead of rising. The present stage of existence is what we share with the lower creatures. Every thing worth having that mankind has ever gained has come from mounting above it. Yet we are always falling back to taking it as an all-sufficient standard, or at least passively letting ourselves be guided by it. It hems us in all round; if we do not put forth power within, it will impress its mould upon us. Its moving powers are pleasure, gain, pride, rebellion. Disguise themselves as they may in plausible shapes, extol themselves as they may as the newest as well as the oldest wisdom, they destroy so far as they prevail. Yet there is no consistent middle course between yielding allegiance to them and accepting sacrifice to God as the shaping influence of our life. Other worthy purposes may seem to lie between; but nothing less than the living, holy, well-pleasing sacrifice can interpret their meaning or secure their rights.

"But be ye transformed," St. Paul continues, "by the renewal of your mind." A sacrifice of the spirit has then preceded all acts by which the body is presented to God. This is what the renewal means. The mind before it is renewed is that mind which lets itself be guided by natural impulses from within, or the average ways of men from without. The mind, when it is renewed, becomes what St. Paul calls the mind of Christ Jesus. It begins its thoughts with God, and refers all things to His will. Thus it imperceptibly transforms, as St. Paul says, the outward life, and the new form which proceeds from it is sacrifice.

I

All life long the change of form proceeds. True
Christian sacrifice is never aimless, never stops short
at itself; it knows nothing of barren self-inflicted
tortures; it is always made that some portion of the
will of God may be done, even as the secret of the
supreme sacrifice is found in the words, " Lo, I come
to do thy will, O God." But then the will of God
has to be followed and learned through every change
of circumstance; and so St. Paul adds, "that ye may
prove (or test) what is the will of God." Here is the
process which makes the divine service of life a
service of reason, laying claim to the ministry of
every faculty which we possess. We have the Spirit
for an ever present Teacher. We have the gospel
to tell us how the will of God was .perfectly done by
the Only Begotten. But all is unavailing save when
we prove for our own selves, aye, and *in* our own
selves, what the will of God is day by day.

Higher than the will of God neither we nor any
being can go; but for all its height, it does not lead
us away from any other standard of worthiness which
experience may have taught us to prize. For, as
St. Paul lastly reminds us, the will of God is itself
identical with all that is good and well-pleasing and
perfect. If, in any field of human interests and
occupations, we become aware of a cause for which
we feel that it would be well that men should strive
and suffer, let us be sure that, purged from the errors
of our imperfect judgment, that cause is part of
God's will. We may choose to fashion to ourselves
in our own minds under the name of God the image
of a Being to whom the ordinary tasks and hopes

and fears of His creatures are indifferent; and then
no doubt the will of God may well seem a distant
unreality, and sacrifice in His name a fruitless and
superstitious folly. But such cannot be the God
who clothes the lilies with brightness and feeds the
hungry ravens. Still less can it be the Father whom
the Apostles knew in His Son Jesus Christ, and the
character of whose will St. Paul invites us to prove
for our own selves.

These then, brethren, are the thoughts by which
St. Paul unites the deepest truths of Christian faith
with the ordinary duties and pursuits of which he
speaks in the two following chapters. If Christ was
not crucified and raised, St. Paul's words become
only heated figures of speech which we cannot long
continue to use in the presence of solid realities.
But if, as we know, his faith was founded on a rock,
then he spoke here in the calm soberness of truth;
then the compassions, the sacrifice, the renewal, the
will of God express the first and greatest facts of our
nature and our doings. If we understand them well,
we are on the way to understand all else well ; if we
disregard them, we inevitably see everything from its
wrong side.

Such also is the voice of Lent. It teaches us
nothing, it profits us nothing, except so far as it
draws us apart to recognize that all our months and
days are built on the compassions, the sacrifice, the
renewal, the will of God ; and arms us with strength
to be true to these hours of faithful and undisturbed
knowledge, when we are once more hurried along
the bewildering stream of outward things. It invites

us to learn for ourselves—the Spirit of God bearing witness with our spirit—what sacrifice means; not only submitting thankfully to the chastenings of our Saviour Judge, but judging and chastening ourselves of our own free will. And therefore it leads us back, for now and for always, to the compassions of God, the compassions of the Cross most of all; mighty, unsearchably mighty, in themselves; mighty also in opening our eyes to recognize the countless compassions in the present which fail not but are new every morning, the changeful tokens of His unchanging faithfulness.

XII

St. Luke's, Lyncombe, Bath, Palm Sunday, 1887.

"BUT that the world may know that I love the Father; and, as the Father gave me commandment, even so I do. Arise, let us go hence."—*John* xiv. 31.

THE fourteenth chapter of St. John's Gospel stands out of the New Testament with a distinctness almost peculiar to itself. Probably no chapter has been so much read even by those who seldom open their Bibles at all. The reason is plain. It is chiefly in times of trouble that we are forced, as it were, to wish to learn what God has to say to us; and this chapter has been felt to be well suited to times of trouble. If we ask why it is singled out by so many when they are in trouble, the opening words give us the answer: "Let not your heart be troubled"; repeated again, "Let not your heart be troubled, neither let it be fearful." Our Lord soon goes off to speak of many things which are not often present to our thoughts when we wish for comfort. Perhaps we do not then take the pains to think very much what those questions of Thomas, and Philip, and Jude mean, or even what Christ's answers to them mean. His own first gracious words go sounding on in our ears. We feel that it is Christ who bids us not to be troubled. We may not be able to know how our hearts are to be delivered from trouble, or what kind of comfort it is that He can and will give us. But we know that His command not to be troubled is in very deed a promise that He is ready to help and heal us; we catch every two or three verses an unutterable gentleness and graciousness in the tone of His words, even when we fail to understand their exact meaning; and we draw some strength from merely resting on Him.

This discourse or conversation with His disciples took place on the night of His betrayal, not many hours before His crucifixion. It is not strange that the shadow of His coming sufferings should fall upon words uttered, as He Himself well knew, so short a time before. The fourteenth and two following chapters are plainly meant as a farewell to the disciples. Words spoken with such a purpose must always have a special fitness for those who are themselves in sorrow or trouble.

But do not let us suppose that this special message is their only message. They belong no less to all men, in joy as well as in sorrow, in the fulness of life as well as in the near prospect of coming death. The heart of the disciples was likely to be troubled not merely because a dear Master and friend was going to die, but because His death seemed as if it

would cut them off from all that made life itself
worth living. They had left all and followed Him.
They had learned that God had work for them to
do; but so long as they followed Him, He pointed
out to them each step they were to take. He was
now going to leave them, and therefore they would
remain by themselves, at once unable to return to the
thoughtless and ignorant state in which they lived
before they knew Him, and bewildered what they
were to do henceforth.

Now this is a kind of trouble which may visit
every one of us: if it does not, perhaps that is a
reason for grief and self-abasement rather than for
rejoicing. The seeming absence of our Lord may
be nothing to us, because His presence is nothing
to us, because we have not yet found out that
we have a Lord indeed. If this is the reason
why our hearts are troubled, we ought to long that
they may be troubled, if so be we may thus awake
to a sense of Him whom we have forgotten. But if
we have indeed in any measure like the disciples
learned to follow Christ, and take Him as the Guide
and Pattern of our lives, we must often be troubled,
when He seems to depart from us, and we seem to
be cut adrift in the wide world, severed, as we fancy,
from that which we had found the very stay and
support of our being. The truth of Christ's unceasing presence with us slips away from us before we
are aware. If He does not force His presence upon
our notice by startling tokens, we are apt to forget
it, and to think that He has forsaken us, when in
reality it is we that have been forsaking Him.

Such a troubling of our hearts may come as easily at one time of our lives as at another : there is no time when we may not take to ourselves the whole teaching here given to the disciples. In other words, we *always* have need of the divine comfort. Comfort itself, in the truest sense of the word, means much more than that fostering and soothing which we often think of as making up the whole of comfort. Comfort means strengthening and support : and what part of our lives is there in which we do not need strengthening and support? We want strength to be given us not only in sorrow and outward trouble, but in the even and unbroken course of our every-day life ; we want it not only that we may be able to stand, but also that we may be able to walk : we want it not only that we may not be conquered by the evils which lie in wait for us beside our path, but that we may ourselves be able to conquer sin and the devil, the root of all the only deadly evils.

Looked at in this light divine comfort is a manlier thing than we sometimes picture it to ourselves. The gospel of Christ, which offers us divine comfort, is not only a wiping of tears and a lulling of pains, though this it is no doubt in part ; but it is the promise of patience and courage and wisdom to enable us to carry on bravely the everlasting fight against the enemies of man, who are also the enemies of God.

By keeping in mind this the drift of the whole chapter, as marked out for us by its first and most familiar words, we shall be best prepared for understanding the force of its last words which form

our text. The last few verses of the chapter bring
us back to that out of which the whole chapter arose,
the thought of our Lord's seeming departure from
His own people. In the thirty-third verse of the
thirteenth chapter He had told them, " Little children,
yet a little while I am with you. Ye shall seek me,
and, as I said unto the Jews, whither I go, ye cannot
come ; so now I say unto you." To St. Peter He
explained more fully that He did not mean that they
could not come at all where He was going ; but only
that they could not come at the same time as He did.
" Whither I go, thou canst not follow me now ; but
thou shalt follow afterwards." And then He went on
to explain that His going away was that He might
prepare a place for them to which they might come
in due time ; and that in the meanwhile He would
not leave them in the lonely, bereaved, helpless state
which they might expect, but would in very deed
Himself come to them, though they might not be
able to press His hand or see His face with their
bodily eyes.

But after all, when all the lessons of wisdom and
greetings of love were spoken, there did remain the
dark cruel fact that He was about to suffer death.
Once more therefore He repeats His cheering
command : " Let not your heart be troubled, neither
let it be fearful." He sums up in the fewest possible
words the grounds of encouragement which He has
already set before them, and then tells them why He
held this perplexing conversation with them. " And
now I have told you before it come to pass, that when
it is come to pass ye may believe." Moreover this

was almost the last opportunity. " I will no more speak much with you ; for the prince of the world cometh." The time was fast approaching when the evil one would be allowed to work his hateful will upon the Son of God, and to inflict a cruel death upon Him. But why was this? Had the evil one any rights of lordship over the Son of God, such as he had tempted Him to confess in the wilderness at the beginning of His ministry? Was there any thing in Him which the evil one could call his own, and through which he could really claim His sub-jection? No, that was not the reason why Christ was going to die. " He, the prince of the world, hath nothing in me : but that the world may know that I love the Father ; and as the Father gave me commandment, even so I do."

Here the disciples were told and we are told why Christ allowed this seeming victory of the evil one. It was to show the world how He loved the Father, and to obey the Father's commandment. These are very simple plain words. They are perhaps not altogether like much that we sometimes hear said by men. But they are Christ's own account of the matter. They tell us part at least of the reason why He thought fit to die.

It is not very strange if we often think of His death as a great and wonderful misery and evil which He underwent, quite distinct from His life and from the acts which He Himself performed. Here we are taught that His death was a part of His life, was one of His acts ; that its infinite worth and importance in the salvation of man come from its

being a free and cheerful deed of the Son of God
Himself.

Once more, it is not very strange if we often think
of Christ's life and death as utterly unlike our lives
and deaths, powerfully affecting them indeed to a
wonderful degree, but far removed from everything
which we have to do or to endure.   But if we
will only listen to Christ's own words, we shall
not find that He spoke of His Godhead or His
sinlessness as making His acts and sufferings as
Man to be wholly of another kind from ours.   Love
of the Father, and obedience to the Father's commands belong to man no less than to the Son of
God.   The law which ruled the death of the only
begotten Son of the Father is the same law which
rules the commonest, pettiest thoughts, words, and
acts of the every-day life of you and me, and of every
one whom we have ever seen or known.

This sounds at first too wonderful to believe.   We
had rather leave God to work out His own mighty
plans in His own way far above our heads, and
wander on ourselves from day to day, rising to no
higher thoughts than the employments which each
day will bring before us.   But we cannot make our
own laws for ourselves.   We cannot utterly crush
out the stamp of God's own likeness which He has
set upon us all, and cut ourselves off from the
purposes which He has designed us to fulfil.   Wonderful as it may be, the only way in which we can be
otherwise than disorderly and wretched is Christ's
way.   And so only can we obtain comfort in time of
need, soothing comfort or strengthening comfort.   In

however many different ways God or man may apply
comfort to us, they all at last come from the same
source, that, whatever we have to do or suffer, Christ
has already done and suffered *for* us in both senses
of the words *for us*, both *instead* of us and also to
enable us to do and suffer ; and that every act and
suffering of Christ came forth from the Father's love,
and was delighted in by the Father's love.

These are the thoughts which are to give us
strength in all that we have to do or to suffer, but
what thoughts are to guide us as to *what* we ought
to do ?   The answer, as we have already virtually
seen, Christ Himself has told us here in describing
His own purpose in submitting to death; love to the
Father and obedience to the Father as the true and
necessary fruit of the love. He had loved the Father
from all eternity, before all worlds.   His delight had
ever been in beholding His Father, and resting in
His Father.   That was no new thing.   He could
not love the Father more than He had ever done,
but He could show to the world how He loved the
Father.   All His life on earth and then His death
were the means by which He showed it to the world.
It was not for His own pride or glory that He
showed it to the world, but that the world might
thereby be saved.   A life of love to the Father was
the only true life possible to any spiritual being.
Christ showed forth such a life that men might
thereby rise to become that which God had made
them to be.   But this love was not a still, unfruitful
repose in the highest heaven.   To be shown to the
world it must come out into the world.   To be a

real love, it must obey real commands. The Son
laid down His life and took it again because so His
Father commanded ; and that obedience became the
redemption of the human race.

Just so is it with ourselves, weak and sinful though
we be. Obedience in the power of that redemption
is the only sure test of true divine love for men as
well as for the Son of God. " If ye love me," says
Christ in this very chapter, " ye will keep my commandments : he that hath my commandments and
keepeth them, he it is that loveth me." It is in the
patient performance of the duties and endurance of
the trials of each day that we prove our fellowship
with the life and the love of heaven itself. Our
Lord's words were turned into deeds immediately.
The last words of the text are " Arise, let us go
hence." From the upper room, where He had
partaken of the Last Supper and spoken these
marvellous words, He at once began His walk
through the city down to the brook Kedron and
the garden of Gethsemane, the agony, the betrayal,
the scourging, and the death. His own heart was
not troubled, neither was it fearful. He bids us
to-day, the first day of the week which we associate
with His sufferings, to arm ourselves with the like
mind, whether it be for life or death. For us as for
Him the path through darkness leads at last to the
upper light. By His resurrection and ascension He
has torn asunder for ever the dark curtain which
bounded the view of men as they looked into the
future. Only let us remember that for us as for Him
strength came less from a future glory than from a

present Father and deliverer.   That was the secret
of the unearthly peace of His words.   In Him we do
but learn more perfectly the depth of the old prophet's
confidence.   " Thou wilt keep him in perfect peace,
whose mind is stayed on thee ; because he trusteth
in thee.   Trust ye in the Lord for ever, for the Lord
Jehovah is an everlasting rock."

XIII

THE PEACE OF CHRIST AND THE PEACE OF THE WORLD

Trinity Church, Stevenage, Wednesday before Easter, 1871.

"THESE things I have spoken unto you that in me ye might have peace."—*John* xvi. 33.

THE last words of the text are those which dwell most in our minds. But if we wish to understand the sense in which the Lord Himself meant them, we must begin at the beginning.

"These things I have spoken unto you," He said. What then were "these things"? They were His last discourse ·on earth, that long conversation, or address (one hardly knows which to call it), occupying four well-known chapters of St. John which followed the Last Supper. In the next chapter, Christ no longer speaks to men, but to God: it is His last prayer and communing with the Father about the work that had been given Him to do. Here in the text we have the close of His teaching to the disciples. He had already been rejected by the world, and ceased to speak to the world. All

through that evening thus far He was withdrawn
from the crowds in the country or the city, and
alone in private with those few who had been following Him as their Master and Lord. What He said on
such an occasion could not be quite like His common
preachings. There must be words fit to be spoken
in the ears of Apostles, which it would have been
worse than useless to have proclaimed aloud in the
temple or on the mountain. It is to these most
sacred outpourings of His heart to those who loved
Him best that He refers, when He says they were
spoken, in order that peace might be had in Him.

But the words spoken to the twelve or the eleven
were not meant for them alone. They were to form
part of the message to be declared hereafter to all
people. They are recorded in our Bibles and read
in our churches to whoever is willing to hear them,
though they are addressed specially to those in every
age who as Christians are disciples of His, learners
from Him. And one great reason why they are
meant for the hearing of all is because they bind
together and give life and meaning to all the other
discourses of Christ which we read elsewhere, spoken
to people of all kinds, to those who rejected Him as
well as those who believed in Him, to those who
hated Him as well as those who loved Him. Every
lesson of the Sermon on the Mount, every parable
will come out to us in clearer light when we remember that they were uttered by the same lips which
bid the disciples' hearts not be troubled or afraid.

Considered in this way the text becomes of more
interest to us than any single verse could be for its

own sake. We are naturally led to ask what is that
great blessing which Christ here wished to give to
those who should hear and give heed to His words.
If "to have peace in Him " is the final blessing of
which He spoke to men before His Passion, it concerns us much to know what that peace is. And
the more we think, brethren, about Christ and His
work, the more deeply we shall feel how entirely
necessary peace, and peace in Him is, if we would
reap the fruit of any blessing which man can crave
and keep it for a lasting possession, or do any work
which can abide.

We all know the two Collects which are read
every Sunday evening after the Collect for the day.
The tender music and calm heavenliness of their
tone must be felt even by a careless ear. The subject of the first and longest of them is peace. We
pray to God, from whom all holy desires, all good
counsels, and all just works do proceed, to give to us
His servants that peace which the world cannot give.
And what are the effects that we look for from
obtaining this peace? That our hearts may be set
to obey God's commandments, that is, that we may
dwell calmly and easily in that temper in which
obedience to God's will seems to us the most natural
thing we can do ; and that being defended from the
fear of our enemies, we may pass our time in rest
and quietness, so firmly fixed on Him who cannot
change, that no shock of outward violence or distress
can bring trouble into our inner hearts. The gift
which we here ask of God is called " that peace
which the world cannot give." The words come,

K

as we all know, from an earlier verse of this same discourse in St. John, the 27th verse of the 14th chapter, " Peace I leave with you, my peace I give unto you: not as the world giveth, give I unto you": and we must dwell for a few moments on that other saying of Christ's in order to understand rightly that of the text.

When He says, " Not as the world giveth," He tells us in effect not only that there are two kinds of giving, but also that there are two kinds of peace; and one of them, be it good or be it bad, He does not profess to give to His disciples.   Distinctions of this kind are familiar enough to our ears and our lips. But it may be doubted whether either speakers or hearers have often any clear and honest understanding of what they mean.   It is not enough to say that the true peace is that which has to do with God and His word and will, and the false that which has to do with earthly things.   Among earthly things our lot is cast by God's ordinance; they are made for our use and enjoyment: if we find them false and deceiving where we have expected to find satisfaction in them, the fault lies not in them but in ourselves: it is because we have cast on them a burden which they were not able to bear; we have rested our whole life upon them, when they were meant as steps to that which eye hath not seen nor ear heard. And again we often deceive ourselves by thinking that we are turning from emptiness to God, when we are merely palled and jaded with a surfeit of pleasant things, and the ways and pursuits of an outward profession of what we take for religion are the only excitements and interests for which we have any appetite left, though our hearts are still wandering as far as ever from Him whose service we flatter ourselves we are entering.

Let us then consider a little how we pass from one thought to the other. So we may learn to prize indeed the true peace which Christ bestows without valuing lightly any other of His bounteous gifts, lesser gifts though they be.

What is the peace which we begin with desiring? Many of you perhaps will say that you do not care much for peace at all. There are many things that you do long for, but not for that. Peace is a quiet thing, and you do not care for quiet. All that is within you, body and mind, is active and stirring : it cannot often be enjoyment to you to be still except when you are tired out, and then the moment your strength is renewed you are eager to be once more in active life and motion. And again, peace is the opposite of fighting, and fighting has its enjoyments. If you are strong, it is a pleasure to you to put forth your strength : a struggle is after all only a kind of game. The pleasure of conquering difficulties is greater than the pleasure of having no difficulties to conquer. Clearly peace of any kind is not one of the blessings most inviting to you just at present.

It is otherwise with those who are of a quieter frame and temper, and with nearly all when they have grown a few years or even months older. Then the promise of peace will have a more welcome sound. The cooling of the blood and the steady work which is necessary to most of us have taught you the value of quiet. You find life quite full enough of troubles and difficulties to take from you most of your pride and pleasure in fighting against them. You would much rather have them away altogether. In other words, you will begin to long for peace. No sooner do you seem to have got clear of one difficulty than another begins to press upon you, and so long as it lasts, you are kept in a constant strain which is only wearisome and vexatious. If you no longer desire pleasures as keenly as you did, you are far more anxious to escape cares and difficulties which lie as stumbling-blocks in your way. Sometimes, nay, very often, this state of things goes on all through life : looking back over our past days we see in them only a long purposeless battle, in which we are content if we have been able merely to hold our own without being utterly beaten down, and we are ready to welcome the cold silence of the grave as offering at least some sort of peace to our poor battered souls and bodies.

But this is not the case with all. Some do seem to find the peace which the toils of your warfare with trouble have taught you to desire. Perhaps after a few years of anxiety and struggle you have worked your way into comparatively easy circumstances, or in some other respects your course has become smoother than before. Sometimes the rest is only for a while, and in a few years another set of difficulties begins. But whether that be so or not, this after-thought still remains always true : do you believe that anyone finds that peace as sweet to his soul when he has got possession of it as it seemed before he reached it? At first it may be so, but how long does the relish remain? No doubt there was weariness in toil and strife, but do you think there is less weariness in the dull vanities of an easy life without high purposes or self-sacrificing affections? Whenever that peace is fairly tried in the balance it is found wanting. It has its value, but what it promised to give is just that which it most fails to give.

We may be sure then that the peace which Christ promises in the text has nothing to do with outward ease and comfort and prosperity. They have a peace of their own, but it is one given by and through the world. Once more I do not say it is an evil peace. It is at last a gift of our Father in heaven, to be received thankfully at His hands. But it is not the peace of the text, the special gift of the suffering Saviour, the fruit and result of drinking in the spirit of His last and deepest discourse. He tells the disciples this very plainly in the same breath. " These things have I spoken unto you that in me ye might have peace : in the world ye shall have tribulation ; but be of good cheer, I have overcome the world." It is well to carry these last words in our minds while we are considering the first half of the verse. The tribulation that is often suffered in the world, and the victory of Christ over the world explain to us the meaning of His own proper gift of peace.

Christ wished to cheer the drooping hearts of His disciples ; that is plain throughout. How was He to do this? Should He tell them that their troubles were but for a few hours, so that when He should have risen from the dead and ascended into heaven, they would suffer no more from the assaults of their enemies, but go happily and peacefully on their way, honoured and popular among men for the sake of their glorified Lord? That would have been no doubt one way of comforting them, a promise of one kind of peace. But the words actually spoken were in a very different strain : " In the world ye shall have tribulation." If they doubted how, supposing that to be so, it was possible for them to receive any peace worth having, let them remember that He had overcome the world. Peace in the conqueror Christ must outweigh tribulation in the conquered world. The saying was still a hard one, for they who judged by the outward eye might wonder what He meant by saying that He had overcome the world. Had not the world well-nigh overcome *Him*? Had He not retreated into the wilderness a few weeks before because there was a plot to take away His life, and was not the attempt sure to be renewed now in the midst of the Passover feast? Yet the words were there, the words of Him who spake as never man spake. And in *all* these words of His lay hid the explanation of both doubts. His victory over the world, His peace which He promised to give, might there be seen to be an inward victory, an inward peace. Peace in the heart is the only supreme all-mastering peace, and the way to it often lies through much tribulation. When all that causes war there has been brought into peace, because all has become loyal to its rightful king, then the war without is little heeded.

Only do not let us delude ourselves into thinking that self-satisfaction, however well garnished with Christian doctrines and Christian phrases, has anything to do with the true peace which Christ gives. There is much contentment in our own doings, or our own faith, or our own love, or our own talk about our own unworthiness, which gives us a kind of placid security, all the more dangerous because it makes believe to come from the gospel.   That is no true peace of mind which does not lead us to ever fresh strivings after a higher life, or which does lead us to despise those who seem to be still entangled in labour and battle.   The peace of Christ is nearer to any other state of mind than to spiritual pride.

Yet another question remains to be asked and answered.   Is the peace of Christ kept only for those who have had a long course of trouble, or who have sickened of outward peace?   If this were so, His promise would be only empty words for the young. They would have to do without His last and best gift.   But this cannot be.   Although it is true that they who have known most of war know best what peace means, yet wherever Christ's Spirit can dwell, there His peace can rest.   Alike in young men and maidens, in old men and children, it has its proper place, though its presence may be known in different ways at different ages.   The peace of Christ is not at variance with any gladness or love of movement and activity, but it keeps that gladness and activity from ministering only to self, and stamps on every look and action a mark which reminds us of man's high calling.   Nor again need it be unknown to

those of older years whose outward troubles are few.
On the one hand, the peace of Christ is not driven
out by toil and care ; it comes from Him who cannot change, and it casts the light of His person and
work on every kind of earthly trouble.   It is in this
the most common lot of men during the greater part
of their lives that its need is felt most, and that it
dwells longest.   But the peace of Christ can also
dwell along with outward peace, and then it brings
life into what was before decaying or decayed.   Great
as are the dangers of ease and prosperity, that peace,
the fruit of His toil and suffering, may be our safe-
guard through them.   In our hot haste we are apt
at times to think peace almost a dead thing, but
when deadness really begins to steal over our own
powers, then it proves itself to be the gift of the
Lord of life by quickening our benumbed spirit.
And if we ask how this can be, let us call to mind
how any kind of real peace, such peace for instance
as comes from human love, has worked within us.
Do we not know already that a restless and feverish
temper takes away all strength from work, all
gladness from pleasure, all comfort from sorrow ?
Without a hidden foundation of quiet peace we are
not really ourselves, we know not whither we are
going.

But those who have felt ever so little the blessedness of peace, above all, of the peace of Christ, must
feel also how impossible it is to describe it in words.
That very name, "the peace of Christ," may teach us
as much as any mere words can.   It is the peace
which dwelt in Christ's own heart while He lived the

life of a man, which His Father gave to Him, and He gives to us.   Surely we have all at some time felt the heavenly breath of its presence as we have read or listened to His words of divine love and wisdom, or remembered how He bore Himself in life and in death.

If this be not so, if the mention of His peace is entirely an empty sound to any of us, and we nevertheless grieve that it should be so, and long to have our share in the blessings which we are told that others have found, we have not far to seek.   Our Saviour's words are in our hands, those words which He says that He spoke with this very purpose that we might find peace in Him, and they tell of a heavenly work in which we are permitted to share. Without those words, or that which is expressed in them, I do not think that any of us have found or will ever find that which we seek.   It is possible for us to school our wild hearts into a steadfast submission to all that befalls us, but He promises far more than this.   We may learn the weakness and folly of loud complaints and violent resistance; we may acquire the habit of keeping in check every hunger of our nature and studying a prudent moderation; we may bear evil days manfully, and not be puffed up overmuch by prosperous days, and yet we may be refusing His true gift.   Great and undeniable blessings, inward blessings, these are; it is folly and wickedness for Christian men to despise them.   They are necessary parts of a Christian life.   But they come short of the heavenly treasures that are hid in Christ.   Nothing but the light of God's love shining in the face of His suffering and conquering Son can transform them into peace, such peace as deserves the name.

The calmest and wisest discernment which does not look above the earth, or at least recognizes nothing beyond but the irresistible might of dim and unknown powers, has yet to learn the beginnings of peace. It dawns on the heart only when we catch a glimpse of the blessed heaven above us, and the ladder which reaches down from above to our feet, and the angels of God ascending and descending.

The promise of the text was given to the disciples just before their Lord's Passion : the thoughts which it suggests, though meant to bear fruit through all their after-life, would be especially needed in those hours of bewildering darkness. Should they be less precious to us now, brethren, when we are in the midst of the week by which that Passion is celebrated ? If we do not need Christ's offer of peace in the same way as they did, if dull indifference to the story of His sufferings is more likely to be the temper of our hearts on these days than distracted sorrow, still our Redeemer's gifts are manifold in their working. The breath of His heavenly peace has no less power to melt the cold languor within us than to drive away fear and anguish. Christ's peace is the peace of life, not of death. Let us take the first step towards it by standing in spirit by His side while the last hours of His mortality are brought before us in the gospel. Let us suffer with His sufferings as we should do for a dear friend, and then let us allow Him to explain to us the meaning

and purpose of that dark tragedy, the Good Shepherd
giving His life for us His wayward sheep, the Son
obeying His Father's will even unto death. And
when the week is over and His Resurrection has
taught us that He is not only stronger than the world
at its worst, the raging throng of blind and sinful
men, but stronger than death itself, the pitiless tyrant
of men ; then let us strive to keep His living image
ever before our inward sight, and so shall we be transformed into His likeness and made partakers of His
peace.

XIV

THE CONQUEROR FROM EDOM

Trinity Church, Stevenage.   Holy Week, 1869.

"WHO is this that cometh from Edom, with dyed garments from Bozrah? this that is glorious in his apparel, travelling in the greatness of his strength? I that speak in righteousness, mighty to save."—
Isaiah lxiii. 1.

EVERY one who comes to church during this week, and asks himself why he comes, will naturally turn in thought to the death of Christ.   Beside that overwhelming event all lesser things shrink easily out of view.   And yet the complaint is heard on every side that the cross has lost its old power over the hearts of men.   There is indeed but too much truth in the complaint.   We need not go far to look for signs of this strange indifference.   We have only to question ourselves honestly, and see whether the stirring of our own hearts at this time is not miserably feeble, a forced and doubtful quiver on the surface when we know there ought to be a shaking to the very depths. There are many things which have their share in bringing about this state of mind, some arising from

our own faults and shortcomings, others from our
being taught or otherwise led to view the cross of
Christ in a very different light from that in which it
stands in the gospel.   And one of these reasons for
our poverty of feeling is just that which we might at
first be tempted to think would have had the opposite
effect, our fear of mixing up the thought of the cross
with any lower thought, our fancy that we are bound
to fix a great gulf between the death of the Son of
God and the rest of His life, much more the lives and
deaths of sinful men.

Holy Week, or as it is also called Passion Week,
the Week of Suffering, here gives us a helpful lesson.
Each of its days looks both forwards and backwards.
The crowning suffering of Good Friday is before us:
we are already within its shadow.   But many of us
know only too well that the scourge and the nails of
the cross are not the only instruments of suffering ;
and Christ Himself was a sufferer long before He
stood in Herod's judgment hall.   Five days of this
week are the end of His ministry as well as the
beginning of His great Passion.   By them we are
led slowly back to the cares and sorrows of that
earlier life when He went about among the people,
healing the sick and casting out devils.   So that
fellowship of His sufferings of which St. Paul speaks
is made easier for every one of us.   Our own common
experience should teach us something of the daily
life of the Son of Man : and from thence we may
mount again through Passion Week to that crucifixion which we grieve to find so strange and distant
from us.

Few even of those who are in the habit of reading the Gospels take notice how large a part of them is filled with the actions of this last busy week at Jerusalem, and the discourses which were then delivered. But if we would prepare ourselves for listening to the teachings of Good Friday in a right spirit, we should carry with us the recollection of the event which stands at the very threshold of the week. The triumphal entry into Jerusalem is very much more than the beginning of the end. At this point the Gospels give no hint of the coming doom. However at variance with custom it might seem for a king to enter his royal city in that lowly guise, still we hear nothing but shouts of gladness and worship, and the whole scene is unlike the quiet and homely ways of Galilee. If we had been among the bystanders, could we have believed that that was in reality a ride to death? Yet so it was; and now we cannot forget what came after if we would. We cannot lay aside the fuller knowledge which raises us above those crowds, and even above the disciples. But let us strive nevertheless to keep before our minds the scene as the disciples beheld it. They saw only in part, yet what they saw was true, true for evermore. Palm Sunday has in it a divine prophecy of Easter, a glory-giving promise that the darkness of death is but a passing shadow. For He who entered the holy city that day was indeed the Son of David, and He rode indeed to victory.

The chapter of prophecy, the first verse of which is the text, seems in some degree to bring together the triumph and the Passion of Christ as they ought

to meet together in our thoughts during these days.
The picture presented to our eyes in the opening
words of the prophet is that of a conqueror returning
from the battle ; His garments are red with the blood
of the Edomites, the old enemies of Israel.   When
asked who He is, and whence come the red stains
upon His dress, He gives an answer which shows
that He is none other than the Lord of Hosts Himself.   " Who is this that cometh from Edom, with
dyed garments from Bozrah ? this that is glorious in
his apparel, travelling in the multitude of his strength?
I that speak in righteousness, mighty to save.   Wherefore art thou red in thine apparel, and thy garments
like him that treadeth in the wine-fat ?   I have
trodden the winepress alone ; and of the people there
was none with me : for I will tread them in mine
anger, and trample them in my fury; and their blood
shall be sprinkled upon my garments, and I will stain
all my raiment.   For the day of vengeance is in mine
heart, and the year of my redeemed is come.   And I
looked, and there was none to help ; and I wondered
that there was none to uphold ; therefore mine own
arm brought salvation unto me ; and my fury, it up-
held me.   And I will tread down the people in mine
anger, and make them drunk in my fury, and I will
bring down their strength to the earth."

The prophet has been cheering his people with
hopes of release from captivity, and return to their
holy city and the land which God had given to be
their home.   But might not Edom, the jealous enemy
of their race, beset them on the way and destroy their
hopes after all ?   Here is the prophet's answer declar-

ing to them the vision which rises before him. He draws away their thoughts from the outward signs and forces of war. They are taught not to boast in their own armies, or dread the armies of their enemy, but to look upward to the unseen Captain of their salvation, to forget their own petty hopes and fears in the eternal counsels of His justice and His love, and to trust in Him with all their hearts as the true undying King of Israel. There is no mark of His having endured any suffering or wound in the battle. The blood which stains His garments is that of the enemy, and not His own. The success is complete, and made plain to all men.

Let us be sure that we learn this lesson well before we go on to the later events of Passion Week. We, to whom the unbroken Bible is given, are taught to see in these doings and prophecies of the Old Testament the types and signs of yet greater wonders in the New Testament. Let us not therefore narrow our vision of the conqueror of Edom when we think of Christ's sufferings and death. Difficult though it may be to our weak and one-sided minds, we must keep before us that ancient form of lordliness and victory while we listen to the story of Him who was despised and rejected of men.

But Christ's gospel forbids us to rest here. It is not enough to know that He is victorious : we must needs learn how and whence comes His strength. "It became him," says the Epistle to the Hebrews, "for whom are all things and by whom are all things, in bringing many sons unto glory, to make the captain of their salvation perfect through sufferings." In His agony and bloody sweat, in His cross and Passion we are taught to see Him winning battle after battle. How it was that He was victorious we may read in every word of His own prayer before the betrayal recorded in the 17th chapter of St. John, when He lifted up His eyes to heaven and said, " Father, I have glorified thee on the earth : I have finished the work which thou gavest me to do ": and yet more plainly in the agony in the garden, when, after praying, " O my Father, if it be possible, let this cup pass from me," He added, " Nevertheless, not as I will, but as thou wilt": and more than all in His last cry in the midst of the darkness upon the cross, " Father, into thy hands I commend my spirit." Such words as these cannot be made clearer by any attempt at explanation. Those will understand them best who most truly bear the spirit of Christ in their hearts, and are willing for His sake and for the sake of His and their brethren both to suffer and to do whatsoever their heavenly Father shall command.

To the outward and fleshly eye that which befel Christ seemed not a victory but a defeat. The Jews who plotted His death, and the Romans who were their tools, fulfilled all their will. He did not even pray that they might not prevail: He only prayed, " Father, forgive them, for they know not what they do." And yet in very truth this was the victory of victories, for it was the victory over the one great enemy of God and man, from whom all enemies in every age have drawn all their evil, all that made them enemies. Only through death could He destroy, or make of none effect, the evil one that had

L

the power of death. The work which was begun, when He refused by commanding the stones to be made bread to put forth a will of His own which was not His Father's will, was finished, when He commended His spirit into His Father's hands.

In the Passion and crucifixion therefore He was not casting away and losing the kingdom which He had seemed to claim when He rode into Jerusalem: He was making it good then and there for ever. The title written over His cross was set up by His murderers in mockery of that claim: to us it is a tenfold more bitter mockery of them and of all who fancy that the spiritual strength of faith and love can be crushed by any tyranny of earthly violence. The power which they thought to snatch from Him who then seemed to be their helpless victim is now bestowed on every man, woman, and child of that human race whose flesh He took.

In that last battle there was once more a conqueror treading the winepress alone; but this time His garments were dipped in His own blood: and henceforward the old vision of the conqueror of Edom puts on a new form. St. John tells us in the 19th chapter of his book of Revelation how he was permitted to look upon it. "And I saw heaven opened, and behold a white horse; and he that sat upon him was called Faithful and True, and in righteousness he doth judge and make war. His eyes were as a flame of fire, and on his head were many crowns; and he had a name written, that no man knew but he himself. And he was clothed in a vesture dipped in blood: and his name is called,

The Word of God. And the armies which were in heaven followed him upon white horses, clothed in fine linen, white and clean, and out of his mouth goeth a sharp sword, that with it he should smite the nations: and he shall rule them with a rod of iron: and he treadeth the winepress of the fierceness and wrath of Almighty God. And he hath on his vesture and on his thigh a name written, King of kings and Lord of lords." When St. John saw this vision of the Word of God, nearly eight hundred years had passed since the old prophet had written: yet every word was true still. Only what seemed like a dream then had now been fully interpreted. St. John had leaned on the breast of Him who wore those raiments dipped in blood, and learned from His own lips the way to conquer every enemy—even the last enemy, death.

And we, to whom a like knowledge is given, must read, with greater awe than any Jew could do, some later verses of the chapter of the text. To him it was natural to think that God would always be on the side of his nation, and fight on their behalf against all that troubled them. Yet hear how the prophet speaks of God's dealings with the house of Israel. " In his love and in his pity he redeemed them; and he bare them, and carried them all the days of old. But they rebelled and vexed his Holy Spirit: therefore he was turned to be their enemy, and he fought against them." These, brethren, are solemn words to us whom God has called to be His children. They tell us that though we belong to Him and He us, we yet may become His enemies.

And the Gospels tell us further that His way of conquering His enemies is not ours. It is not only when His hand lies heavy upon us, and we are hard pressed by sorrow or distress, that we should turn and consider our ways. When we are going our own path and thinking little of Him, the thing that ought to frighten us most is that we meet with so few hindrances. Perhaps when we begin wilfully to break His laws, we wonder whether He will punish us, and more than half fear that He will: but, when no loss follows, we grow bolder by degrees, and at last actually feel a dreadful pride in thinking how well we do without God, and how cunningly we contrive to break His commandments without being the worse for it. So dreamed the Jews who crucified their King. Their success seemed complete. They thought, every one thought, they were having it all their own way. But they were frightfully mistaken. From that day the doom of their nation was sealed.

Let these thoughts remind us that Passion Week has yet another character. It is the last week of Lent. When Ash Wednesday came, how many sins did we not think we would break off? and how many have we really put away since then? As the weeks slipped noiselessly by, have not most of us remained as dull and lifeless as before, disposed to gamble, as it were, with God, and run all the risks of going on as we have always done? If the thought of Christ's Passion and death and His unconquerable love to us therein revealed, has in anywise awakened our drowsy thoughts of better things, let us thank God that the holiest hours of Lent, few though they are, are still before us, and strive by His grace to use their help in breaking the bonds of our one true enemy.

He who triumphed over the tempter on earth is now looking down, watching the struggle in many a heart, which longs for a better life, yet dares not trust itself to a service which means the daily giving up of self. His voice, if we will but hear it, still speaks to us, joyfully welcoming every conquest over evil passions, and inviting us ever onward to surer and more enduring victories. " I know thy works," He says, " and thy labour and thy patience; how thou hast borne, and hast patience, and for my name's sake hast laboured and hast not fainted." This is well, but this is not all. He bids us press forward as He did. There is work to be done as well as trial to be endured. " To him that over-cometh will I grant to sit with me in my throne," such is the marvellous promise of the Prince of the kings of earth, who loved us and washed us from our sins in His own blood, and hath made us too kings and priests unto God and His Father: " To him that overcometh will I grant to sit with me in my throne, even as I also overcame, and am set down with my Father in his throne."

XV

NEWNESS OF LIFE

Sherborne School Chapel. Easter Day, 1885.

"THAT like as Christ was raised from the dead through the glory of the Father, so we also might walk in newness of life."—*Rom.* vi. 4 (R.V.).

OUR Lord speaks to us by His resurrection with a voice which has a power of making itself heard, and making itself felt, at every age of life and every stage of experience. No child of Christian parents can have the thought of death as an actual dark fact brought before his mind, without having its darkness in some measure lightened for him by his having learned how God's only Son our Lord, who was crucified, dead, and buried, on the third day rose again from the dead. As years go on, and knowledge and experience widen, and thought grows more active, we come to learn how much more is wrapped up in that one mighty event than we had dreamed at first; for the message of Easter is indeed the one foundation of all rational faith, and of all sure and sober hope. In its first simplicity, in the form 'God hath raised His Son Jesus from the dead,'—this was what made the Apostles new men, and sent them forth to live and to die proclaiming it to others, and thereby to begin that wondrous change in men's thoughts and deeds by which Christendom has arisen. Believing this, we have the keystone which fits into and holds together all the upward thought of man, all the recognition of a living and loving God above, without which the seeming order of the world is found to dissolve at last into unmeaning disorder and dreary ruin. Believing this, we hold a sovereign remedy against all repining or discouragement about ourselves or about the world around us. Christ is risen : however strong be the powers of evil, One stronger than they lives, and lives for evermore.

But there are other secondary lessons through which our Lord's resurrection is brought nearer, as it were, to our daily lives. One such lesson is taught in the text, a lesson specially in harmony with the tone of our Easter services, and not less specially fitted for a time when the Confirmation is still but lately passed, and the thoughts which it inspired cannot have yet lost all their freshness.

In the text St. Paul teaches us to keep our Lord's resurrection before our minds as a pattern, if we may venture to say so, after which we are to strive to mould ourselves and our conduct, and a power by which we may be enabled to do this. Let no one think for a moment that St. Paul is here only playing with words, and tracing fanciful resemblances between things that really have no connection. The idea here set before us is one which is deeply rooted in the apostolic teaching in various places, and it is expounded here in various forms of language through several verses. Here, as so often elsewhere in the New Testament, we must bear in mind the greatness of the change through which men passed in the apostolic age when they became Christians. Their entrance into the Church of Christ's disciples made their former life to be as a former state of existence. The governing motives within were new, the habits and doings of the society to which they belonged were new. Of this great change the baptism which completed it and sealed it remained thenceforth a vivid and impressive image. The plunge beneath the waters of the river was as the swallowing up of the old life. The rising up out of the waters was as the ascent from a tomb into the new life. The intervening moments during which they were hidden from the eyes of men, the moments which divided the renounced past from the welcomed future, might well be thought of as a kind of death, now that Christ's resurrection had made it possible and even natural to think of death as a passage between two lives, a lower life and a higher.

This was however but half the truth which the Apostles taught. The Christian's passage through the symbolic death of baptism not only bore a likeness to Christ's own passage through actual death : it was also an entrance into the closest personal connection with that unique death and resurrection. To become a member of Christ's body was to become a sharer in all that was His, in all that befel Him. These of course are difficult things to speak of or to understand : we can as yet lay hold of only a part of what they mean. But we must not on that account turn away from them as though they did not concern us. We must rather lay ourselves open to receive the Apostle's teaching, and believe that the Spirit, which enlightened him to see deep things of God, will in due time enlighten us also through the experience of a Christian life.

The sixth chapter of the epistle begins with an indignant protest against the suggestion that the freedom of God's grace may make it a reasonable thing for a baptized Christian man to go on sinning, just as he had been in the habit of doing as a matter of course in his heathen days. " Are ye ignorant," St. Paul asks, " that all we who were baptized into Christ Jesus were baptized into his death ? We were buried therefore with Him through baptism into death ; that like as Christ was raised from the dead through the glory of the Father, so we also might walk in newness of life." All through these and the following verses the same two threads of teaching are twisted together into a single cord. St. Paul bids the Christians of his day treat the life in which sin was, as it were, natural and at home as a life past and done with, cut off from the present by the death-like passage through the waters of baptism, so that the present life was a new life : and again he lifts this new life of theirs into a higher world of power by bidding them call to mind their membership in the living Lord who had Himself passed through the most literal death, and whose resurrection was now working within them towards all things high and good.

We Christians of a later time have no old life of active sin before our baptism to look back to, as most of the converts of the Apostles had ; so that St. Paul's language receives no such clear explanation from our own experience as it did from theirs. The ancient baptism which crowned the repentance and faith of converts of ripe age is now for most of us divided into two parts, our baptism in infancy and our confirmation in youth, as better suits the changed circumstances under which we are brought up. Our years before confirmation have not been spent in a heathen society, but in Christian families and Christian schools in the midst of Christian people. St. Paul's words therefore are not in their most obvious sense natural for us to use. Yet their truth remains unchanged even for us, though to us they speak it as it were in a parable. That heathen life of the early converts before baptism sets vividly before us the state into which we all, Christians though we be, are at every moment ready to sink, whenever we lose our hold on God—the old man within us, as St. Paul elsewhere calls it, the corrupt self which turns its back on conscience and is led by low desires. That is the life renounced in baptism : the truer and better life of which baptism is the promise is a new life indeed. All that is good within us is the fruit of some renewal. The baser nature which we share with the brutes is there within us from the first. God's own image, the heavenly seed, is likewise there, but it has to fill and subdue the baser nature if it is not itself to be extinguished, and this filling and subduing is a renewal. Every time that we cherish a high aspiration, every time that we resist a low temptation, we are treading under foot the old and merely natural self, and walking afresh in newness of life.

And on the other hand whenever any one of us so walks in newness of life, he is not entering on some strange and solitary course, but simply doing that which should come naturally to him as a Christian, simply acting as befits one who belongs to the congregation of Christ's people. He is not alone. He is a sharer in what is greater than himself. The great new life which came into the world when Christ was raised from the dead is his, and is all around him. He is the heir of all that it has wrought in and for mankind during eighteen hundred years, and the receiver of countless present influences by which it lifts and stirs men's hearts to-day.

But there is another sense in which St. Paul's words may be rightly applied to our own experience. Hitherto we have been considering what is meant by walking in newness of life in contrast to the old heathenish life, the old natural life in the lower sense of the word 'natural,' which was renounced for us once for all in baptism, and which those of us who have been confirmed have renounced anew in our own names. Besides however this great single fundamental entrance on newness of life, which in part lies behind us in the past, and in part is spread over our whole lifetime, there are lesser times again and again repeated, when an opportunity is given us of entering into newness of life in such a manner that St. Paul's words may well sound in our ears with something of their literal and original force.

Every now and then, if our hearts are not utterly hard, we are led to pause, and be still, and think over our own past ways, and resolve to make a fresh start in well-doing. Sometimes the occasion may be some outward event in our own life or the life of those most dear to us, sometimes it may be some fresh impression on our inner selves, arising from words spoken in our hearing, or words flashing upon us in a book that we are reading, or the mere thoughts suggested by some incident which has reached our ears. Whatever the occasion may be, if it has had any good results, it is because it has stirred up a resolve to walk in newness of life. Much is often said, and most truly said, of the value of quiet steady patient growth in well-doing as opposed to a hasty and merely impulsive movement by fits and starts. But it is also true that our progress, when we make any, is made by steps, and that at each effectual step there is a looking back on all our past as a forsaken life, a life so darkened by recollections of shame that we are thankful to cast it, as it were, behind us, that we may go forward in newness of life. Of course in so doing we need not be blind to any attainments in well-doing which God's good Spirit has granted to us, to any progress, however imperfect, which we may have already made. This would be untrue to fact, and nothing can justify untruthfulness in our inward discourse with ourselves any more than in our outward intercourse with others. But in like manner we cannot doubt that the converts of the apostles' days remembered good thoughts and words and deeds belonging to their heathen days, inspired by Him who is the Author of all good in every man, although they knew that in embracing the faith of Christ they had been passing from darkness into light. For them and for us, whatever be the good intermixed with the evil of the past, whatever the evil intermixed with the hoped for good of the future, every fresh desire and effort for better things must begin with a breaking of the yoke with which hardened habits of sloth and evil have bound us.

Besides these new beginnings which are unexpectedly from time to time brought near to us by the overruling providence of God, the regular course of the seasons supplies us with other resting-places which invite us to the task of renewal. Such, we all know, are the beginnings of new years, either the years of common usage, or those personal years on which we enter through birthdays. But we do not sufficiently remember the more frequent intervals by which our heavenly Father mercifully breaks up for us the steady flow of time, and so helps us to make renewal the unfailing habit of our hearts and minds. Each time that Sunday begins a new week, the occupations of the last six days are laid aside, and the space of rest itself invites us to pause and look backward and look forward. If we bear in mind the event which Sunday as a Christian festival commemorates, we shall hear it week by week inviting us, in the name of our risen Lord, to bury in His grave our own past life with all its failures and sins, and rise up afresh in His strength to serve Him with a new spirit in new devotion. The remem-

brance of this, the most wonderful of God's countless
wonderful works, will come back to us each week as
an old memory to which the days last lived have
given an unexpected newness, helping us to understand things that would otherwise bewilder us, showing them to be works of a Lord who is indeed
merciful and gracious, and whose glory is shown
alike in giving life and in restoring life.   If such are
the thoughts which each Sunday morning awakens
in us, the public worship of the day, together with
the opportunities which the day gives for private
thought and prayer, will be welcomed as hallowing
the new resolve, and strengthening it in its first hours
with power from on high.   And so the work-days
which follow will be divided off from the work-days
behind by a glimpse of personal communion with
the Lord's resurrection, enabling us to enter with
renewed and uplifted hearts on their familiar employments and temptations and encouragements.

But this is not all.   We have not to wait even
from Sunday to Sunday for divinely sent interrup-
tions of our heedless and self-indulgent ways.   Each
time that night gives place to morning, and the
sky is filled anew with light and the earth with
the life which the light awakens, and we ourselves
rise refreshed out of darkness and sleep, have we
not an image, and more than an image, of the new
life to which we may rise out of our buried past?
Is not each day as a little separate life which sinks
at last in darkness?   When we wake in the morning,
do we not feel that, after the death-like sleep which
has restored our jaded faculties, it is as it were a new

life that we are beginning, and not merely a new
portion of our former life? And if so, have we not
here a true and fitting starting-point for a solemn
and vigorous awakening of all that is within us to a
newness of moral and spiritual life? The Father,
who raised His Only Begotten from the grave to
which He had descended for our sakes, restores us
each morning to meet another day, and blesses
our entrance upon it. As the well-known hymn
reminds us :

> " New every morning is the love
> Our wakening and uprising prove ;
> Through sleep and darkness safely brought,
> Restored to life and power and thought."

And the answer which we His children can make is
in like manner a renewal of our love to Him, and a
consequent renewal of all our thoughts and ways.

For each one of us the renewal must take place
first in the depths of his own heart : no one else can
bring it to pass for him. But as he goes forward on
the divine way, he will more and more find himself
strengthened with the sense of fellowship with others.
There is no loneliness like that of selfishness, and
every step that is taken towards a new life is also a
step towards the joy and pride of brotherhood. Of
this we have a pledge in the festival of Holy Communion in which many of us joined this Easter
morning. In that sacrament we hold communion
at once with our risen Lord above, and with the
members of His church below. Those who partake
of it together in this chapel confess by so doing that

they are united by sacred bonds one to another, and through one another to all other members of the school, and to all who are set over it. In the presence of such a fellowship all evil passions are put to shame, the sense of being alike sharers in a work which is part of God's work swallows up the littlenesses of daily routine, and the walking in newness of life is seen to carry with it the increase of mutual confidence and goodwill, making itself felt in the instinctive acts of cordial help and service which again in their turn give force and reality to the love of God and the service of God. On the one hand its promise is of life and of resurrection which is the renewal of life ; on the other it points back to the cross, and so to the death unto sin, the mortification of all evil desires, which is the first step in the renewal of life. It thus echoes back in another shape the trumpet voice of the Easter anthem by which St. Paul carries on and completes his teaching in the text : "Christ being raised from the dead dieth no more ; death no more hath dominion over him. For the death that he died he died unto sin once : but the life that he liveth he liveth unto God. Even so reckon ye also yourselves to be dead unto sin, but alive unto God in Christ Jesus."

XVI

FAITH IN THE RESURRECTION THE FOUNDATION OF ENDURING WORK

Emmanuel College Chapel, Fifth Sunday after Easter, 1880.

"THEREFORE, my beloved brethren, be ye stedfast, unmoveable, always abounding in the work of the Lord, forasmuch as ye know that your labour is not in vain in the Lord."—1 *Cor.* xv. 58.

THESE words close the marvellous chapter in which Christ's rising from the dead is set forth as the great fact without which the gospel would be no gospel at all, and in which His return to life is declared to be the promise that we too shall rise again. That chapter passes through several changing moods of feeling. In it St. Paul sometimes argues, sometimes delivers a message as with authority from above, sometimes tells what has already happened, sometimes declares beforehand what is yet to come, sometimes almost fiercely rebukes, sometimes cheers with stirring words of encouragement. Towards the end he rises into an exulting hymn of praise. Beyond that we might think he could not go. We

might expect him to leave off there on the highest
stretch of uplifted feeling. Or if he in writing his
letter had reasons for not pausing there, we might
think that at least the Church in her burial service
might well have broken off there, and sent forth
the mourners with that song of triumph ringing
in their ears as the last sounds heard before they
leave the house of God. But no! St. Paul does
not stop there, and the Church does not stop there.
Calmer and quieter words follow, words of encouragement but also of command, which lead our
thoughts back and away from the sorrow of the
present and the hope of the future, and fix them
on the work of this present life which still lies
before us who remain.

Some of us will probably remember that our
Easter Collect takes a similar turn at its close,
and some too may perhaps remember having had
a feeling not unlike disappointment at its taking
this turn. They have had an uneasy check, as if
they were somehow let drop to a lower level in
the midst of the prayer, so that it almost seemed
to lose its Easter character. It begins with lofty
words about the great event itself, and the great
future which it declares to us: " Almighty God,
who through Thy only begotten Son Jesus Christ
hast overcome death, and opened unto us the gate
of everlasting life." That is what God has done
for us: next, what do we ask Him to do for us
now as the fittest benefit for us to desire in connection with such a glorious commemoration ? Simply
this : " We humbly beseech Thee that, as by Thy

special grace preventing us Thou dost put into our
minds good desires, so by Thy continual help we
may bring the same to good effect." It is hardly
possible, when we begin to think about the meaning
of the prayers we repeat, not to be struck here by
the seeming fall from great things to small. But
this very startlingness of the change of tone should
lead us to inquire whether we have really understood either the first part of the Collect or the
second.

It is, to begin with, a striking fact that this
change of tone is found alike in St. Paul and in the
Collect. There is no reason to think that the Collect
was merely taken from the lesson. They have not
a single important word in common; and even when
we look at the sense, the one is far from being a
mere echo of the other. They who wrote the Collect
must have shaped its prayer by nothing except by
the thoughts about Christ's resurrection, which had
come to them in the depth of their own hearts. Not
in carelessness or in slackness of feeling did they
leave for our use the petition at which we so easily
stumble. They had, it is more reasonable to believe,
a keener sense than most men of the bitterness of
present sorrow, a firmer and steadier hope than most
men of coming glory; but above all a clearer insight
than most men into the power of Christ's resurrection, into what it has bestowed on man, and into
what man must sooner or later become if he were
robbed of its assurance.

Leaving the Collect for the present, let us go back
to the text. The previous verse renders thanks to

God, who gives the victory through Jesus Christ our
Lord. What then is the victory? Who are the
enemies that are triumphed over? First, death and
the grave; next, sin, and the law as the strength of
sin. To outward appearance the victory of death
and the grave over *us* is clear and unquestioned.
Sooner or later death lays us all low. We may
build up for ourselves a great fortune, or we may
gather together rich stores of wisdom. But death
comes at last, and to all appearance we let fall
everything for which we have been labouring all our
life long and pass into nothingness. So it is if the
full term of life is allowed us. But we all know that
with many death and the grave claim their own
much earlier. A child is snatched from its mother's
arms; or sickness wastes out of life one whose course
is but half run; or a sudden stroke lays low the
strong man in the midst of his vigorous life. The
power of man may well astonish us sometimes, to
such heights can it rise; but it shrinks into nothing
at the touch of death. Nay, we suffer cruelly from
the victorious power of death long before it comes.
The dark shadow rests on our whole life, though it
is long before we become aware of it. We all do
our work as under sentence, knowing that the difference between one and another is only of a few years.

Once more, what makes death most terrible is the
sense of sin, which happily few or none can quite
escape in a Christian land. So long as sin means to
us the angering of an unknown God, and death the
passage into an unknown world, these two unknowns
make each the other more awful. Sin is then the

sting of death, because death seems likely to be an approach to Him whose presence we have shunned on earth. In that state of mind He is known only as a law-giver. The word which comes forth from Him seems to do nothing but forbid and hinder and imprison and bind, and no living creature can thrive in such a world of unmixed restraint. As St. Paul says, the law becomes the very strength of sin. Happily even under the Old Testament no such gloomy image of the Most High ever presented itself to any true Israelite. The very law given by Moses came from One who had brought His people not into, but out of, the house of bondage. Still in later days it became harder for any one who believed in God at all to rejoice in the light of His countenance. St. Paul knew only too well by what had passed in his own soul not only how death received more terrible strength from sin, but how sin and death together were enabled to vex him before, when God appeared to him only as the author of commandments which it was not possible entirely to keep. He had known from childhood what psalmists and prophets had taught of the loving-kindness of the Lord. But all that had come to sound as mere words. He had felt that the victory lay with his enemies, and life was for him distracted and harassed by the misery of his powerlessness to resist.

But all was changed when, after assisting at the murder of Stephen, he came to believe in Stephen's Master. In Jesus Christ he saw One who, while fulfilling the law, had lived a holier and better life than any law could possibly command; One whose

delight was to do His Father's will, in whom love
did more than all the work of duty, love to the
Father whose glory He made known to men, love to
men, perverse, ungrateful men, whom He came to
save.   But Christ had not only overthrown the
bondage of law; He had done no sin, neither had
guile been found in His mouth.   He had shown
that the only perfect way to resist evil was to follow
good.   These were some of the fruits of His life and
of the death of suffering which crowned it.

Thus the work of Christ's life was imperfect
while death remained unconquered.   This triumph
too was won by His resurrection.   He did not
resist death.   That which would have slain others
slew Him.   He died as any other man would have
died.   But that first Easter morning saw an empty
tomb.   God raised Him from the dead, and so
caused victory to pass from death to man.   Man
must go through death as the Son of man had done,
but death became known as the gate of everlasting
life.   Life on earth remained a struggle, a battle;
but one that it was possible to wage to good effect
now that hope brightened the way in front.   One
who bore the flesh of man had grappled with all the
dark spectres which destroy the freedom of living by
freezing and chilling the blood.   The power of them
all was made known to be but for a time.   Their
conqueror was ever living to help His feebler brethren
as they struggled on towards their goal.

But that which made victory most sure was the
unveiling of the face of God above.   His Son in
every act of His ministry had been destroying some

bitter fruit of sin and death, healing the diseased,
feeding the hungry, bringing comfort to the sorrow-
ing, cleansing the unclean, bringing good news to
those who thought no good news possible, and so
showing the true mind of the Lord and King of
men ; while at the same time He had shown no
paltering with evil and had called on all to be
perfect even as their Father in heaven was perfect.
In the wonders of His cross He had displayed the
Father's love in the only way in which sinful and
suffering men could understand its depth, by the
sacrifice of life itself as the last step in the willing
endurance of torment.   And then by raising Him
from the dead God had shown that life is *the* gift
which He designed for men, and that He can turn
all the evils of our mortal state into steps to His
glory.

Hence it was that St. Paul could fitly pass from
his hymn of victory to the sober voice of exhortation
which speaks to us in the text.   The tyranny of
death and sin had made the life of men on earth
distracted and torn.   The victory bestowed in Jesus
Christ gave it back peace and order.   The holiest
were still stained with sin, and had to sorrow for
their own shortcomings.   But they could strive with
hope, now that they knew their sins were not against
a tyrannous taskmaster or a fateful law, but against
a Father who corrected them that He might train
them into His own likeness.   Death and all the
lesser evils and miseries of life were still there,
still grievous to mortal flesh and blood : but they
rather helped to build up life on surer foundations

than to shatter it; for henceforth there was fellow-ship in sufferings between brethren on earth, and between them all and Him who had led the way; and death could be looked at steadily, and at last, when it came visibly near, even with joy, since it led not into an unknown darkness, but into another mansion of the Father's one house.

" Therefore, my beloved brethren," writes St. Paul, "be ye stedfast, unmoveable, always abounding in the work of the Lord, forasmuch as ye know that your labour is not in vain in the Lord." The power of the resurrection is here in each word. There is nothing which might not have been said by St. Paul at any other time; but here alone has each idea its full force. He speaks not to a set of men to whom it was natural to be contending against each other, each striving to grasp and hold what he could against all comers, each jealous and suspicious of the other as at best a possible enemy. Their faith in a common Lord has made known to them that they are brethren, beloved alike by the Apostle to whom they owed so much. He bids them be steadfast and unmovable. The assurance of victory in Christ was not a thing to intoxicate them, and send them wildly rushing hither and thither shouting for joy at the unspeakable gift. It was meant to be used as a remedy against the diseases of their spirits. Its great effect should be to steady them, leading them to say quietly, as the Apostle himself did, " I know him in whom I have believed." Passion should not shake them, ambition should not shake them, greediness of gain should not shake them, grief should not shake them, fear should not shake them. Not that they were to harden themselves against any emotion not sinful, but it was not to make them swerve from their course : it was to be consumed within, and kindle and purify the inner fire.

We may often hear it said in the present day that our Christian faith concerns only another and distant life, whereas what men need from a faith is that it should exercise power over them and their doings in this present life. Nor can it be denied that this sort of language finds much excuse in a way of thinking and speaking which is only too common among Christians. But it is entirely untrue as applied to the Christian faith as believed and taught by St. Paul and the other Apostles. Nowhere in the New Testament is the resurrection to a future life so largely spoken of or so strongly insisted on as in this great chapter of 1 Corinthians, and yet the lesson drawn as the conclusion of the whole is a lesson about the work of the present, about steadfastness in work, unstinting energy in work, hopefulness in work.

The future and the present were linked together in St. Paul's mind by the thought of the eternal and ever-present God, who brings forth the future out of the present. In St. Paul's eyes all work done by any single man in his short span of life, nay in his every year, in his every week, in his every hour, could be rightly understood only as a part of God's great work, or else as resisting God's work. To him all the duties and relationships of life were the means by which God is working out His purposes for mankind, and the true spirit in which each man should work was that he should thankfully regard himself as permitted to contribute his portion to the all-embracing work of God. Those therefore to whom he wrote were to go forwards not as though in a work of their own or for themselves, but in the work of the Lord, recognizing each man his own place and his brother's place in the great field, and helping each other so as to lighten the labour and carry on the work ; even as St. Paul had said earlier in the epistle, " We are labourers together with God : ye are God's husbandry, ye are God's building." And again they were not only to do God's work, but to be always abounding in it. The work of the Lord was not to be done by fits and starts, taking turns with self-seeking for profit or for pleasure, but always as the one true blessed business of life. They were to abound in it, to let it flow over in the cheerful bounty of a willing mind. It was not to be done scantily, with close reckoning of thus much and no more. They were not to be thinking how soon they might give up doing the work of the Lord, and turn to other work for themselves. This grudging and bargaining temper was altogether out of place in men's dealings with God, whose gifts are all gifts of free grace, and whose work draws into itself all human work that is work indeed and not vanity or destruction. In making His work their one object in life, putting duty in the place of self-seeking in all things, they would be in the one right way, and find that He takes better care of His children than they can ever take of themselves.

Last comes the encouragement, the holding forth

of the hope that will have power to kindle within them steadfastness and constant abounding in the work of the Lord. Let us mark well what sort of hope it is. It is not a hope of pleasure or happiness, or anything of that kind. It is simply this, " Forasmuch as ye know that your labour is not in vain in the Lord." The work is the Lord's, St. Paul would say, the labour is yours; but it is not vain labour. No one who has any manhood in him can ever think labour in itself a hardship. Few things worth doing can be done without labour; and on the other hand labour is necessary for the moral and spiritual health of our own inward selves. But it is no less true that there is nothing so disheartening as the feeling that labour is in vain. While we look only to the outward appearance, we must often have this sad and damping fear. The world is full of chances which thwart our best chosen plans, and bring them as it seems to nought. Then death comes perhaps when we seem to have only just begun, at all events long before we have made all secure. So the labour of a life appears to be well-nigh or quite lost, and on a smaller scale the same experience appears to repeat itself day by day. Not so, St. Paul would bid us remember, if we have faith in Christ's resurrection, and in all that is involved in it. That declares to us that seeming death is the beginning of a better life, seeming failure the first and necessary step towards a more perfect success. The new life, the new success may be in outer shape unlike anything that we have dreamed; but they are not the less true. Now that He has conquered death for us, that victory enables us, nay commands us, to look on all human doings with quite other eyes.   While it deepens all responsibilities, it lights them up with the vision of heavenly purposes and heavenly powers.   No labour done in the Lord, as by willing and loving servants of a loved and trusted Master, without eager anxiety to seize on credit or on profit for ourselves, but with simple readiness to do a part, though it be the humblest in the great joint work—no such labour is ever lost. It bears fruit to life eternal: fruit not seldom in the outward growth of the divine kingdom; fruit often in the spirits of others who see what we think God alone sees; fruit always in the training and ripening of our own spirits towards greater likeness to God and more helpful service of men.

And now, brethren, shall we say that such an exhortation as this is not a worthy ending to the great chapter of the Resurrection when read over one of our own dead?   Does it not exactly meet the wrong state of mind which is so natural and yet so hard to correct?· The hours and days that follow death, especially when it comes in a startling form, are apt to be full of a great awe and wonder, which presently dies away into common thoughts and leaves no trace behind, just as it started up in the midst of a life in which serious thoughts had no place.   These strong and sudden differences of feeling, violent fits in the midst of a long indifference, have little divine about them.   They do not make grief deep and true, they do not make the hope of God's glory bright and strong, they do not cause the unseen world to

put forth a true power over our daily lives.   As
Christians, brethren, not death but resurrection is the
true object of our remembrance.   To be steadfast,
unmovable, always abounding in the work of the
Lord is not only the true lesson for daily practice,
but the true comfort in sorrow when sorrow comes,
the true remedy for indifference.   Only by labouring in the present as servants of a redeemed Lord
can we build up the glorious future.   In communion
with Him and with our brethren His gift of life is
offered freely to all, life to be employed for His own
work, a work that must go ever forwards throughout
the ages of eternity.

XVII

THE PERPETUAL PRESENCE OF CHRIST

Emmanuel College Chapel, Sunday after Ascension Day, 1875.

"Lo, I am with you alway, even unto the end of the world."—
Matt. xxviii. 20.

THESE are the last words in St. Matthew's Gospel,
that Gospel which, on the whole, gives us the fullest
picture of our Lord, His words, and His deeds, and
which supplies to most readers of the Bible the
greater part of their impressions about Him. The
words were spoken by Christ at one of the few
recorded times when He appeared to His disciples
after His resurrection. It is plain from the account
given in the first chapter of Acts that these cannot
have been Christ's very last words, but still they
belong to those last forty days of His appearance on
earth between His rising from the grave and His
mounting up into heaven; and St. Matthew plainly
regarded them as a true ending to His whole story,
the weightiest part of a solemn charge which marked
that all was nearly over.

When the two Maries came to the tomb, St. Matthew tells us, on that first Easter morning, they found it empty. An angel sat by the door. He bid them fear not, for He whom they sought was risen. He invited them to look in and see the place where the body had lain; and then he sent them off with speed to tell the disciples the joyful news, and to command them to hasten into Galilee, where they would find Christ gone before them. As the Maries were on their way to the disciples, Jesus Himself met them and greeted them; He bid them not be afraid; He repeated once more the angel's message which they were to give to the disciples, calling the disciples by the now familiar but then new and striking name, "My brethren." To Galilee the eleven Apostles went. We may gather from St. John's account that in the meanwhile He had twice appeared to them. But now, by a special command, they were to meet Him for a purpose known to Himself. A strange journey it must have been to them. A few days before they had entered Jerusalem over the Mount of Olives, surrounded by crowds shouting "Hosanna to the Son of David." Yet that day must have seemed an age ago, so filled up was the time between with stirring and wonderful discourses of their Lord, and at last with yet more exciting events—the Betrayal, the Trial, the Scourging, and the Crucifixion. Now the Lord was once more alive; He had sent them a loving message inviting them to meet Him. But what a place He had chosen for the meeting! No longer at Jerusalem, where men thronged for business or politics or pleasure or religion, the holiest spot in Israel and the wickedest, now made more unspeakably holy for them as the scene of His death and His triumph over death. Not at Bethany, the little village at the other side of the hill, where for the first four nights of the week before His death He had lodged at the friendly house of Martha and Mary and Lazarus. He chose now to meet them in their own country, Galilee. There at the beginning of His ministry He had found them busy with their fishing-boats and nets, and commanded them to follow Himself. There on a mountain, perhaps the same mountain now appointed as the meeting-place, He had called them to Him, and sent them forth to preach the kingdom of heaven, to heal the sick, raise the dead, and cast out devils. Sometimes with Him, sometimes without Him, but always with the feeling that they belonged to Him, they had for months laboured there at the same work.

And what was the new charge and teaching? "All power is given unto me in heaven and in earth. Go ye therefore, and teach all nations, baptizing them in the name of the Father, and of the Son, and of the Holy Ghost: teaching them to observe all things whatsoever I have commanded you: and, lo, I am with you alway, even unto the end of the world." The early part of this charge I must pass over to-day, except so far as it bears on the last words. Christ bid the disciples go forth to teach and baptize all nations, because all power was now given to Him in heaven and in earth. That is, if ever they had been accustomed to find help and encouragement in feeling that they were working with Him, much more should they have confidence now, for all power was given Him in heaven and in earth, and He was with them as much as ever, with them always even unto the end of the world. In like manner we read at the end of St. Mark how, after the Lord had spoken unto them and had been received up into heaven, they went forth and preached everywhere, the Lord working with them, and confirming the word (*i.e.* the word which they preached) with signs following.

Let us now consider a little what was the meaning of this promise of Christ to be with them always. Did He mean that having now risen from the dead He intended to live on earth among them in their sight for evermore? Was it that He proposed to begin once more His old life, and merely carry that on without ceasing unhindered by the malice of His enemies? If any such thought entered their minds, they were soon undeceived. Not many days later, as we read in the Acts of the Apostles, when He was once more among them on the Mount of Olives, after He had done speaking, He was taken up and a cloud received Him out of their sight, and from that time they beheld Him no more.

Was He then mocking them when He told them that He would be with them always? Sometimes they might be tempted to think so. Yet if they looked back, they would see how all things had been leading them to a truer understanding about His presence, and about all His dealings with them. Just six weeks before He had said that He was

N

going away from them, but would return to them. In a few hours He had indeed gone away, or rather, as it seemed, been taken away. Not in the midst of peaceful converse with them on the lonely mountain, not mounting up towards the sky and received into the depths of a bright cloud. His departure had been in all things the reverse of this. He was nailed to a cross in the presence of all the people, the Jewish priests who had plotted His death, the Jewish people who had shouted and rejoiced at the sight, the Roman soldiers whose hands had done the cruel deed. His side had been pierced with a spear, and blood and water came forth, the signs of death. No angel had appeared out of heaven to save Him. He had gone away from them, as it seemed, utterly and hopelessly. His body had been laid in a tomb hewn out of the rock, hidden away from the sight of men. Yet on the second morning He had burst the bonds of death and of the grave; He rose, and came back and appeared once more among them. Thus once already His words had come true when He promised to return, and return seemed impossible; so they might well believe that in one way or another the promise would continue to be fulfilled.

Since the Easter morning His appearances among them had been few and strange. For days together, as far as we know, they saw nothing of Him. Suddenly He would appear in the midst of them, converse graciously with them, and as suddenly vanish. Evidently His bodily presence was another thing from what it had been. When that last time He disappeared out of their sight in a cloud, there was

hardly anything more wonderful than at the other
times when He suddenly ceased to be visibly present.
Those earlier vanishings seemed as though meant to
prepare them for His final concealment. Thus by
slow degrees He was as it were weaning them from
converse with His mere face and voice. But in all
this there would have been but a melancholy sort of
kindness, if He had not been helping them to an ever
increasing warmth and depth of converse with Himself, with that in Him of which face and voice were
only the outward signs. When we speak of knowing
a person well, being intimate with them, it is not
their looks or their words that we mean. We may
be familiar with the looks and words of people to
whom we know that we are all the while in the
truest sense strangers. The looks and the words
are great helps towards knowledge ; without them
we should seldom be able to succeed in knowing
our friends. But we are all yet well aware that
the thing which we properly know and love is
behind, that it cannot be touched, or seen, or heard.
And this thing in Christ, the true Christ Himself, it
was that He was trying to fix more and more deeply
in the hearts and minds of the disciples. Every word
and deed of His which they understood helped towards this end ; and the assurance carried by strong
impressive words like those in the text, words that
demanded to be thought about and deeply considered
before they could be received, came with clinching
power to quicken the difficult lesson.

We too, brethren, require to be taught the same
truth no less. Every week we repeat in the Creed

that Jesus Christ, God's only Son, our Lord, ascended into heaven, and sitteth on the right hand of God the Father. On Thursday last we celebrated the feast of the Ascension. We mean by this nothing less than that Christ left the earth on which He once dwelt. There was a time when He lived like you or me, when He had a body with face and limbs like ours, when like us He hungered and was fed, was weary and slept. But all came to an end at last. After His rising from the dead He departed from the sight of men as completely as if He had lain for ever in the tomb. And yet to us men living here on earth, accustomed to know each other's presence by our bodily senses, He says, " Lo, I am with you alway, even unto the end of the world."

As the Apostles stood gazing up at the blank cloud which had hidden from view the ascending form of Christ, two angels announced to them that He should one day come in like manner as they had seen Him depart. But this assurance has nothing to do with the promise of the text. That speaks not of a return after absence, but of a perpetual presence.

Again, Christ had promised to send to them from the Father the Holy Ghost the Comforter, that He might abide with them for ever. Ten days after the Ascension the presence of the Holy Ghost was declared by new and marvellous gifts of speech. Yet this too was no true fulfilment of the text. It was the Christ whom they had known in the body that was to be with them all their days.

Yes, brethren, it is He and none other who is with *us* all our days. We have not known Him in the

body by our own eyes and ears, but we may know
Him in the body, if we please, by the eyes and ears of
those who walked with Him on earth. If Jesus were
living and working in some other country at this day,
and friends of ours were there and wrote to us letters
describing exactly what they saw and heard from
Him, should we not feel that that was the next thing
to being on the spot ourselves? Yet that is very
nearly our case now. A story that was true when it
was first written does not become untrue by being
kept eighteen hundred years. Our Gospels are like
letters written for our learning by those who had
walked and talked with Christ, or conversed with
those who had. God knows that we are creatures
of flesh and blood, that our knowledge of others
begins through flesh and blood, and needs that foundation for its growth in higher things. He does not
call on us to believe in the presence of a stranger, of
one whom we can only catch at by dim guesses of
thought. If Christ is not familiar to us by the acts
of His very hands, by the words that came out of
His very lips, the fault is ours. The Gospel stories
bring us into the very presence of those acts and
those words. And if they have touched our hearts,
if their holiness and love have stirred in us a true
feeling of our own unworthiness and His wondrous
grace and mercy, we have already begun to know
Him not after the flesh but after the Spirit, we stand
in His presence, in some measure, not face to face,
but heart to heart.

If this be so, then the barriers of our earthly state
are broken down. Though Christ departed from the

world of eyes and ears so many ages ago, there is no reason why He may not be present to our inner selves now. Nay, not only *may* be present but *must* be present, if He is still living. Can we suppose that that Lord and Saviour, whom we have felt drawing us to Himself by the magic cords of His divine Spirit, has grown weary of being with men all their days? We believe that, though He died once, He is alive for evermore. Does not that turn the answer of our own heart to the grace and truth which once lived in Jesus of Nazareth into a glad welcoming of His presence now? Thus the text passes from being a bewildering riddle into the most natural of all truths.

We finish now the line of holy seasons which we have been following since Christmas. At Christmas we were led to think of the Son of God stooping to men, bringing down heaven to earth, restoring new life to the worn-out races of men. Now we look back on His finished course. His ascension is the lifting up of man whose nature He took, the raising of earth to heaven, the promise of a better life than the earth at its best can give. His presence with us now proclaims not only God with us but us with God. He does not bid us hate or despise this lower world in which we daily dwell. He teaches us that we do not know it or value it half enough, that we waste and befoul its best possessions because we are so little thankful to Him, so greedy to snatch or filch them from our neighbours. But He teaches us yet more to lift up our thoughts and desires to the heavenly world of peace and love, and be content with no lower portion than God Himself as our joy and our rest.

XVIII

THE BIRTHDAY OF THE CHURCH

St. Ippolyts. Whitsunday, 1867.

" BUT unto every one of us is given grace according to the measure of the gift of Christ. Wherefore he saith, when he ascended up on high, he led captivity captive, and gave gifts unto men. . . . And he gave some apostles, and some prophets. and some evangelists, and some pastors and teachers."—*Eph.* iv. 7, 8, 11.

TWO birthdays, and two alone, are known to the Christian faith. As Christmas day is the birthday of Christ, so Whitsunday is the birthday of the Church, of that great society of men which He intended should in some sense present towards the rest of the world the image of Himself after He had ascended into heaven, and which the Apostles called His body.

This part of the message of Whitsuntide is commonly forgotten. In thinking of this season as speaking to us of the coming down of the Holy Ghost, we are apt to remember only the work which the Holy Ghost carries on in the hearts of each single man. It is well indeed that we should bear in mind always how every Christian has a right to look on the Holy Ghost as his purifier, his own comforter, his own guide.   But it is not well that we should forget the yet greater work of His which is set before us in the story of His descent on the day of Pentecost, the work of binding men together in one Church, and teaching each not only to guide himself aright, but to fulfil his particular task for the good of all the rest.

We may read this lesson very plainly in the account given in the Acts of the signs that accompanied that great outpouring of the Holy Spirit. The sounds of many different languages were then heard spoken, yet all alike spoke the wonderful works of God.   Of the causes of separation between man and man that lie in difference of language and race, and in strangership generally, the Church was declared to be conqueror on its very birthday.   The power which prevailed in a single temporary sign was the power of the Holy Ghost.   That power filling the hearts of men, and quickening them with unheard of heat and life, a heat and life so great that foolish bystanders said they were full of new wine, came forth at the same time in a manner which showed that henceforth the worship of God and His Christ would break down all the old hindrances to brotherly feeling which came from differences of blood and speech and custom.   The Spirit of Him who had died for all mankind alike was seen overriding the oldest and strongest causes of separation. Henceforth each nation was not to have its own religion, its own gods.   For all alike there should be

One God the Father, One Lord Jesus Christ, One
Holy Ghost the Paraclete. Men might still go on
nursing their old suspicions and jealousies, even
though they called themselves Christians ; but those
who really suffered their Christian faith to inspire
them, those who followed the leading of the One
All-uniting Spirit and knew themselves to be members of an Universal Church, could not but treat men
of other tongues from themselves as still fellow-
citizens and brethren, members of the same great
commonwealth in heaven. The sin of man has
indeed from a very early time sadly hindered this
work of the Spirit. Evil thoughts and passions have
not ceased to inflame the minds of Christian nations
against other Christian nations, and the old passions
of barbarism seem to be now breaking forth anew :
we are as yet far from completing what the day
of Pentecost began. But, in word at least, the
Church is still true to that first declaration of its
duty, repeated every time we repeat the Litany,
praying that it may please God to give to all
nations unity, peace, and comfort.

Again, other barriers hardly less powerful than difference of language and race are spoken of by St.
Paul as broken down for members of the Church.
" As many of you," he says, " as have been baptized
into Christ, have put on Christ. There is neither
Jew nor Greek, there is neither bond nor free." In
those days, when servants were commonly slaves, and
slavery was usually full of hardship and cruelty, it
seemed the strangest of dreams that master and
slave should feel themselves to be brethren, should

worship the same Lord.   Yet this was an early work
of the Church, an early fruit of the descent of the
Holy Ghost.   We have only to read St. Paul's short
Epistle to Philemon about his runaway slave Onesi-
mus, to see how true and wonderful was the change.
Of this runaway slave St. Paul writes to his master,
" Perhaps he therefore departed for a season, that
thou shouldest receive him for ever; not now as a
servant (or slave), but above a servant (or slave),
a brother beloved, specially to me, but how much
more unto thee, both in the flesh and in the Lord."
Here too, no doubt, the work remains incomplete.
Slavery is gone from most Christian lands, and the
Church has had no small share in destroying it.
But even where there is no slavery there may be,
and there are, other false relations of class to class,
there are contempt and insolence on the one side,
grudging and hatred on the other.   Yet still the
Church by its doctrine, and in some measure at
least by its practice, carries on the spirit which
shone so brightly in St. Paul.   Its services know no
difference between one or another: all may kneel
side by side to eat of the same bread and drink
of the same cup: and the best cure of social evils
is still to be looked for in a deeper sense of our
Christian fellowship, and a greater eagerness to take
our proper places as members of the same body.

Another way in which the Spirit called forth the
mutual goodwill of the infant Church is described a
little further on in the Acts.   " The multitude of
them that believed," we are told, " were of one heart
and of one soul; neither said any of them that ought

of the things which he possessed was his own, but they had all things common." " And they continuing daily with one accord in the temple, and breaking bread from house to house, did eat their meat with gladness and singleness of heart, praising God, and having favour with all the people." As far as we can judge, the having all things in common was never practised except at Jerusalem, and did not last long there. No doubt it was found a better plan to improve the ordinary ways of society, and set high examples of duty and devotion in them, than to bring in a new state of things which could not work well as soon as any of the members became lukewarm and half-hearted, and thus ready for such hypocrisy as that of Ananias. But not the less was that possession of all things in common a striking sign of what the Church was meant to practise and to teach, the dependence of all the members on each other, and the faith that every man is bound not to live for himself and his own comfort and benefit, but for the help and service of his fellows. The Church went back to private property; but it never went back to the unchristian doctrine that a man may do what he likes with his own. That picture of the early Christians eating their food with gladness and singleness of heart, praising God and having favour with all the people, seems as if it belonged to another world, so unlike is it to the state of things with which we unhappily are most familiar. But such was the natural life of men who believed in earnest that God had made them, that Christ had redeemed them, and that the Holy Ghost was binding them together in a holy brotherhood: and such, brethren, will be our natural life, when we too embrace that belief with our whole hearts, when we exercise membership of the Church in deed and not in name.

To every one of us, says St. Paul, is given his grace according to the measure of the gift of God. Each one of us has his own place: none are unplaced. Each one has a work to do for God and man: none has a right to be idle or to work only for himself. And as God has set us our place in the world and our work, so He also gives us our grace, our special portion of the universal Spirit, our help from above, that we may continue in our assigned place, and do cheerfully and well our appointed work. The various works, the various graces make up one great scheme. The one Holy Spirit looks upon all the manifold doings of the world as a general might look on his army. He sees and knows exactly what has to be done, and how, and when, and by whom. He does not work by Himself but through us. He does not set us each to work by himself but through others. The work is not rightly done unless all act together, the one employed on this, the other on that; each knowing that his own share is but a small part of the whole, knowing that his own power is but small, but looking for answering help and support from the willing labour of others; rejoicing where he can feel that he is standing shoulder to shoulder with them, glad to feel the comfort of their presence, not less glad to bring his own efforts to their aid as an offering of goodwill.

When Christ ascended up on high, He led captivity captive : He conquered all the evil powers that till then had kept man in bondage. It was the finishing of His Easter victory. He conquered death and the fear of death, death of the body, death of the spirit : He conquered sin and the debasement which sin brings. He broke all the bonds which hold men fast in slavery ; among the rest these bonds which keep them apart from each other, of language and race, of rank and wealth, and every other. Good and useful in themselves, they had become bonds through the devices of the spirit of evil, and he had striven for mastery with Christ and not prevailed. And now from heaven Christ gave gifts to men, good gifts, best of all the gift of the Holy Spirit. When we say in the Creed, " I believe in the Holy Ghost," we go on " the Holy Catholic Church." The two beliefs hang closely together. The effect of the Holy Spirit's teaching is to make us feel that we are members of the Church, not single atoms struggling for our own private good or salvation, but fellow-workers in a mighty host. If the Holy Spirit dwells in our separate hearts, still more truly does He dwell in the whole Church as one body, breathing into all its members His own gifts of life and love.

St. Paul goes on to point out some of the special offices in the Church which He ordains and inspires. We might fancy that all the work of the Church in that day was to be done by great Apostles like St. Paul or St. Peter or St. John, men who had seen Christ after His resurrection, and were looked up to everywhere as rulers, carrying with them something of His personal presence. But no : they had their work to do, and grace given them for the doing of it. But the Church had need of others too. Christ gave not only " some apostles," but also " some prophets," men who saw deeper into the meaning of Scripture and the will of God than their neighbours ; who had a peculiar power of uttering words which seemed to come out of heaven itself. Again, there was need of " some evangelists," missionaries, as we should call them, specially fitted for going about from place to place and spreading the gospel among the heathen. Still more was there need of " some pastors and teachers," men in charge of fixed Christian con-gregations, whom it was their duty as pastors to guide, and as teachers to instruct. To each was given his office, to each his grace to execute his office.

These words, brethren, have a peculiar interest for us this Whitsuntide. On Tuesday next, Whit Tuesday, which is also St. Barnabas's day, the festival of the first apostle or bishop who was chosen by men instead of by Christ Himself, our new bishop is to be consecrated to his office in the cathedral of this diocese. We are not accustomed, most of us, to think often of the bishop, partly because, having the charge over more than six hun-dred parishes, he cannot be seen among us except now and then at a confirmation, or on some such occasion ; partly also because we are apt to forget the Church to which we belong. Yet, as we have been seeing to-day, to forget that we are members of the Church, and to neglect the duties which that

membership brings, is to throw away no small part
of the Bible's teaching, no small part of the spiritual
blessings which God has provided for our use. The
bishop's office, placed as he is over more than two
counties, should remind us that we are neither single
Christians merely, nor a single Christian congregation merely, but parts of a great Christian body
which is held together inwardly by the Spirit of God,
outwardly by the office and authority of our bishops.
Looking back through the sixty generations which
separate us from that great day of Pentecost, and
feeling bitterly how far we are removed from the faith
and love of that early day, the thought of our bishop
may still help us to believe that one unbroken Church
stretches from that time to this, since he is but the
last bearer of an office of which we see the beginning
there.   Some of us at least will, I trust, think on
Tuesday of the duty laid on him towards us all, and
find comfort in so remembering that we are a part of
the great communion which was born at the first
Whitsuntide.   But as God gives him a work to do
with us, so does He give us a work to do with him.
All have their part in it, for all are members of the
Church.   Christ has appointed the clergy for one
kind of task in His Church, He has appointed the
laity for many others.   Each one has religious duties
of one sort or other, but there are many duties not
called religious which may still be done in the spirit
that belongs to members of a church, the spirit which
St. Paul describes by saying that "whether one
member suffer, all the members suffer with it; or one
member be honoured, all the members rejoice with

it." Remember how he repeats that greater than all
the spiritual gifts which men suppose to be the sole
concern of the Church is what he calls charity, the
temper which makes men seek not their own, bear all
things, believe all things, hope all things, endure all
things, because they have learned from Christ the
blessedness of caring for others and seeking the good
of others. There is room for this true charity in
every word we utter, every action we perform.
When we show it in our daily behaviour towards
all whom we have to meet, we are doing the greatest
of all the work assigned to the Church. The true
power of the Spirit, the true faith in the Church of
Christ is shown not so much in destroying differences
between one man and another, as in finding in them
finger-posts to the different kinds of work which have
to be done in the world. When men of different
nations and languages feel that each country can best
serve God and all other countries by being faithful to
Him in its own character, the Church is fulfilling its
task, the Spirit is prevailing. When men of different
ranks and stations in one country, or the different
members of one family, accept heartily the places
marked out to them by God as given them that they
may bring in each his share to the common welfare,
the Church is fulfilling its task, the Spirit is prevailing.
But the beginning and ending of all these things is
the love and fear of God, and thankful remembrance
of the salvation wrought out by His Son. Whitsuntide comes after Ascension, the last of the seasons by
which we have been tracing our blessed Lord from
His cradle to His cross and grave, and from His

grave to His Father's right hand.   By following
Him with all our hearts and souls, and suffering
Him to fashion us into His own likeness, we become
partakers of His Spirit, and discover our fellowship
in the glorious Church of His redeemed.

XIX

VICTORY OVER THE WORLD

Great St. Mary's, Cambridge, Fifth Sunday after Trinity, 1875.

"WHATSOEVER is born of God overcometh the world, and this is the victory that overcometh the world, even our faith. Who is he that overcometh the world but he that believeth that Jesus is the Son of God?"—1 *John* v. 4, 5.

THESE two verses ring in all our ears as if they meant something very great. What is the greatness there? Is it only the music of a favoured Apostle discoursing about high and heavenly things, music that touches us and uplifts us for the moment by its unearthliness, yet not a thing which we can seize and keep for ordinary use? Or is it the greatness of strong and simple wisdom, which we can turn to practical account always if only we can find out what it means? The question answers itself the moment it is fairly asked. We may be willing in our lazy, careless way to listen to the text as if it were only a string of beautiful words from a very holy man. But we cannot think that the true account of the matter, if we pay the least attention to St. John's tone. There is no mark of angelic dreaming there. He uses none but the weightiest words, and they fall one after another like the blows of a well-aimed hammer. Clearly he was in terrible earnest himself, and only anxious to carry his earnestness unbroken and uncooled to the hearts of his people. He was speaking what he knew; and what he knew was just that which it most concerns us to know. It sounds a bold thing to say, but it is strictly true, that he knew more about our own every-day affairs than we do ourselves; that is, his knowledge of them was more to the point than our own knowledge; he could tell great things from little better than we can; and if we can but follow his lead in the great things, we shall find the little will take care of themselves.

Men of the Old Testament, filled with the Spirit of God and looking calmly back over all that they had felt in themselves and seen in others, declared in few words the lesson which they had found the most true of all, "The fear of the Lord is the beginning of wisdom." That famous saying can never lose its truth. There is that in all of us which requires the grave restraint of the fear of God. At the beginning of life especially, when everything looks bright and we are rejoicing in the sense of freedom, we cannot do without that check to keep us from turning all our acts into play, and very mad and dangerous play too. As soon as responsibilities begin, the need of wisdom begins also. Choice lies before us, and we have to learn how to choose—to choose what are the right things to aim at, and then again to choose

the best way to reach those right things.   If we go
by haphazard instead of choosing, or if we choose
perversely and badly, that proceeds from want of
wisdom.   Wisdom is not to be won all in a day, and
we often have to buy it dearly.   Its lessons have to
be gathered here and there from many different
kinds of experience, but the beginning of it is the
fear of the Lord.   To start with that is to start on
the right road, the road towards which all things
turn their true faces.

But as we get on in life, we feel more and more
the want of other helps besides wisdom.   Clouds
come over our sky.   Almost every year seems to
bring some fresh hindrance to keep us from doing
what we would.   The world, which looked at first so
rich in sources of enjoyment, proves to be full of
things which have power to hurt us too.   Enjoyments themselves grow stale and lose their savour,
or we have no longer time or means or spirit to
enter into them; and meanwhile the pains and
troubles increase.   Some of them may visit us now
and then only, as bodily suffering and disease, or
grief of mind, while others seem never to depart, as
the weary fretting cares of a dull and laborious life.
So also it is with the hindrances.   At first the world
seemed like a wide, open playground, on which we
could follow our likings in good measure and run
freely where we pleased.   Now we find ourselves
hampered as soon as we begin to stir.   We are too
like prisoners, able only to pace a few steps within
the encompassing walls, and in each of those steps
feeling the weight of their chains as they move.

Now when we want to give a single name to the
source of these pains and hindrances, do we not say
they come from the world? do we not complain that
it is a hard world, a rough world, a cruel world, a
weary world? Some of the pains and hindrances
evidently have their birth in ourselves, our own
bodies and minds; we may have brought them on
ourselves by our own sin or folly, or they may have
fallen upon us without fault that we can discover of
ourselves or of any man. Other pains and hindrances come from the sky or the earth, from God's
creation in short, which has within it powers that
destroy as well as powers that bless. But most of
our troubles and most of the checks upon our liberty
are owing to our fellowmen. It is them we have
chiefly in view when we complain that the world
presses us hard. We are apt to think that every-
body around us has nothing to do but wait upon
us and make things easy for us. We find on the
contrary that we have to suffer partly from their
indifference, partly from their ill-usage. They are
covetous and grasping, or jealous and spiteful, or
false and cheating, or cruel and tyrannical, or else
they are at least too wrapped up in themselves and
their own affairs and enjoyments to trouble themselves about us when we greatly depend on them.
We very often fancy these things when they are not
really true; but very often also they are true. Much
less than we suppose of our difficulties is owing to
the fault of others, but still others are answerable for
a great deal. If our fellow-creatures did their duty,
many a bitter pain and many an oppressive difficulty

would leave us at once. We do suffer every moment of our lives, one and all of us, from the oppression, and the unjust oppression, of the world. The fact itself is true, though it is no warrant for hatred and scorn.

Yet we must be madmen before we could think the world wholly evil. If it presses us hard, it also furnishes us with all or nearly all that makes life possible. If our fellow-creatures daily vex and hinder us, we yet hourly live by their help. Our dulness and thanklessness and fondness for a grievance hide this fact from us. But it is true; just as true as that other fact of the world's ill-usage of us. We could as easily strip the flesh off our bones as strip ourselves free from family and neighbours. It is only by wilful forgetfulness that we can ever look on our world as wholly an evil thing. Rather it is mixed of good and evil. Some of its evil, its worst evil, is apt to beguile us by a false appearance of good; for the world which we have to renounce is the world approaching us as a false friend rather than as an enemy, though it is as an enemy that the text leads us to consider it to-day. And in so doing, as I said just now, we must regard the world of human beings around us as mixed of good and evil. In our wiser moments we may see its value and necessity; but it is full of twists and crookednesses, and so we come naturally enough to look upon it as an enemy, and to strive to resist it at all points. The effort is vain. It is useless to kick against the pricks. We do but pierce and bruise ourselves still more. We make no real progress towards freedom.

Some time before Christ came, that discovery had been fully made by most of the wiser of mankind. They felt the yoke of the world as the bitterness of an enemy. They knew at the same time that violent resistance was useless. How, they asked themselves, could something like a free and happy life be obtained? The answers to the question, however different they might sound, were all in much the same strain: men resolved to calm down all strong and active feeling, to deaden and numb all pleasurable and painful feeling. They laboured to draw themselves close within themselves, and leave no tender point for the world to fasten on and wound. Where it pressed they made up their minds to give way; they were willing to do anything rather than provoke a conflict. Instead of trying to bend the. world to themselves, they bent themselves to the world. So they hoped to escape being overcome by the world, or at least not to be crushed by it. They had their reward. If they parted with all great happiness, they escaped much misery. But it was a poor existence at best, a wilful half-death of soul and body. And meanwhile other men in the world were left to shift for themselves. Those who were avoiding conflict for their own sakes would hardly expose themselves to rough blows for the sake of others. Meanwhile the. world itself grew from bad to worse. All the corruption and falseness and violence within it became every day more rank and deadly.

We are now, I trust, prepared to understand part at least of what St. John had in his mind when he spoke about overcoming the world. You will observe this phrase occurs no less than three times in the text. St. John takes for granted that his people's desire is to overcome the world, and so in three different forms of speech he shows how this conquest has been won and may always be won. The steps which most of us take are those of which I have already spoken. We begin by not seeing that there is any world at all in our way. Then after a time we feel its power to vex us, and we rebel against it : in our own fashion we try to overcome it, and we fail : we find it to be stronger than we are. Then we are apt to fall back in a sullen way: we challenge battle with the world as little as we can, content if only it does not quite overcome us; but we chafe under its injuries, and the sense of them casts a gloom over every view that meets our eyes, and embitters all our dealings with others.

If to stand on this footing with the world satisfies us, we may let the text alone. It has then no clear message for us to hear. But who is there that does not long for freedom from the world's bondage, when once he has felt it galling him? Now this deliverance is what St. John offers. From the day that Christ rose from the dead a new prospect opened on man's dealings with the world. Not to escape being overcome by the world, but to turn round upon the world, and overcome the world became the Christian's glory and the Christian's duty. Easter morning had melted away the darkness which hung at first about the Master's words, " Be of good cheer,

I have overcome the world," words spoken, let us remember, just before the betrayal, the judgment, the scourging, and the death on the cross. To our own first wild way of resisting the world Christ never gave the least encouragement. He let the world treat Him as it liked, and at last put Him to death. Not till the Father raised Him from the dead was it seen that the world had had no real power over Him, in short that, as He said, when the prince of this world came to seize the prey, he found he had nothing in Him. Each step that the world had taken to crush Him had become in God's hands a step forward in the completion of His work and the advancement of His kingdom.

Whatsoever is born of God, says St. John, overcometh the world. We bring with us into the world an earthly and animal life which sets us upon seeking our own pleasure and pride and gain. When God's light shines into our hearts so that we can see Him in His perfect goodness, not shutting Himself up in lonely glory, but ever working at the saving of mankind, then a new life which is a part of His life, born of Him, begins within us. In our feeble way we begin to learn to imitate His ungrudging love. The feeling of sonship to Him takes the lead of all other thoughts and desires. We strive simply to follow His will, whether it brings us into conflict with the world or no. If it does, we go straight forward and let the world do its worst upon us. It cannot use us worse than it used God's Only Begotten. That which it can overcome, except it be by our own consent, is only our flesh. Our spirit, caught up into communion with the spirit of God, does but renew itself by the trial. It conquers for itself by gaining fresh strength for fresh victories. It conquers for others by the life and hope which every suffering borne for God spreads all around.

The next words of the text show whence comes this strange power which turns defeat into victory. It is no mere imitation of God by man as a painter might copy a dead picture. It is faith, simple unreserved trust in the Father above, the willing joyful hanging with the whole heart upon Him, the desire to be emptied of all that is of self, and to be filled only with His Spirit of holiness. What that power can do and will do one day we little dream at present. But St. John reminds us what it had done already in his day. It had in a wonderful manner already overcome the world. "This is the victory," not literally "that overcometh," but "that overcame the world," he says. When Christ hung on the cross and all had forsaken Him and fled, God's kingdom seemed to have lost all that it had once gained, and to have shrunk into that one single dying form. When He had ascended into heaven, a little band of helpless fishermen and their friends stood alone in the midst of a world that thirsted for their blood. We see the promise of the triumph of their faith in their rejoicing that they were counted worthy to suffer shame for Christ's name. By the persecution after Stephen's death the world thought to destroy them ; and so it would have done, if their faith had failed and they had consented to give up or hide their devotion to their true Lord. But no; it was the world that suffered defeat. They were

spread throughout Judaea and Samaria, and carried
with them the word of life ; out of that very persecution sprang the conversion of St. Paul, the
mightiest of all God's instruments for spreading the
gospel of His Son. So it was time after time :
all who held fast the faith of Christ endured as
seeing Him that cannot be seen ; and when St.
John wrote, every country in the civilized world
had within it a company of men who with no
earthly advantage to gain, and often at the cost
of ruin and torture, had shown the powerlessness
of the world when putting out all its cruellest
strength to resist the advance of faith.

But the text teaches one lesson more concerning
this faith. Faith of any kind in one above us, God
or man, is mighty. But the faith which had done
these wonders had a character of its own ; it was
our faith, the Christians' faith, the faith of them
that believe that Jesus is the Son of God. The
one certain means of keeping faith in God strong
and pure is to fill the heart with the image of
Jesus of Nazareth, His doings, His sufferings, and
His glory, while we hold fast the firm belief in
Him as the only begotten Son of God. If He
was no more than a man, the picture merely tells
us how devoted to God, how willing to suffer for
men one of ourselves can be. God Himself in that
case would still remain hidden in darkness ; we
could but guess whether He cared for us, or was
indifferent to us, or hated us : we should, to say
the least, enjoy none of the full light which the
gospel throws upon His mind towards us. And

in that case how hard would it be for us in this age of the world to trust Him wholly! We are always prone, far too prone, to think ill of any one whom we feel to be above us ; to take for granted that, where there is power, it will be used unjustly and unmercifully. None can have the faintest suspicion of such a mind in God, while he believes God's Son to have been Jesus of Nazareth : he who believes that must see how He, the very Father's image, used His power ; how it was the glory of His strength to become weakness, of His pride to be lowly and despised, of His fulness to empty Himself of all, of His life to submit to death ; and all this for the sake of His rebellious creatures. The very essence of faith lies in this, that it draws heaven down to earth, and fills the heart of the faithful with power from on high. But it is Christ alone who brings heaven within reach of earth : without Him every year that the world grows older, the abyss between earth and heaven becomes more and more hopeless to cross. When He is believed in, heaven enters into earth and earth into heaven, and the faithful fighter against the world can see everywhere around his daily path sure signs of the presence of the Lord in whom he trusts.

But the Christian victory over the world has in it much more than that victory over the world of which we dream at first. As Christ came not into the world to condemn the world, but that the world through Him might be saved, such also must the Christian's triumphs be. He has to conquer not for himself but for his Lord : he has to be ever winning

back for the Lord's side some part of the world
which is now against Him. He must believe that
faith is the gift of God which He is ready to bestow
on all men that are in the world as much as on
himself. He can never therefore think of them as
enemies whom he is to hate, however he may feel the
stress of their enmity to him. " Father forgive them,
for they know not what they do," must be the prayer
ever on his lips for the stupidest and most malignant.
The world has not let go its grip upon us so long as
we have any lurking hatreds and jealousies remaining
behind. When faith grows ardent enough to con-
sume all such personal and private passions, then
we gain a fresh victory both for ourselves and for
God. And the further we advance, the less will it be
possible for us to think of overcoming the world for
our own sake. The zeal against the world, which
begins in the mere impulse to break its bondage
over ourselves, is lost at last in patient endurance
of all except what stands in the way of the heavenly
kingdom. Yet this progress is gained without chilling
a single strong or warm feeling for fear of giving the
world the opportunity of hurting us. All our feelings,
whether the possession of them brings us delight or
suffering, are God's gifts to us to be used in His
work. We can spare none of them in our lifelong
battle with the world. They are part of the arms of
our warfare. Sometimes it is by a great joy that
God lifts us forward, and then how should we have
fared, if we had killed in ourselves the power of joy ?
Sometimes it is by a great sorrow that He draws
us closer to Himself ; and then how should we have

been able to yield to Him, if we had killed in ourselves the power of sorrow? Nothing too that can bring us into sympathy with any living creature can we afford to waste. If we believe that Jesus is the Son of God, we must patiently use His means for drawing others to His service, knowing that so we shall be best doing our part in preparing the day when the kingdom of the world shall become the kingdom of our Lord and of His Christ.

XX

THE DESIRE OF THE FLESH NOT THE DESIRE OF THE MAN

St. Ippolyts, Fourteenth Sunday after Trinity, 1857.

I.

"I say then, Walk in the Spirit, and ye shall not fulfil the lust of the flesh. For the flesh lusteth against the spirit, and the spirit against the flesh: and these are contrary the one to the other: so that ye cannot do the things that ye would."—*Gal.* v. 16, 17.

"WALK in the Spirit, and ye shall not fulfil the lust of the flesh," says St. Paul; that is, "You will be able to avoid fulfilling the lust of the flesh, if only you will walk in the Spirit." How did he know that they wished not to fulfil the lust of the flesh? Or, taking the counsel as addressed to ourselves, is it certain that we wish not to fulfil the lust of the flesh? These are questions which have to be answered if we want to understand either what St. Paul meant, or whether what he said is of any use to our own selves.

Some will say at once that the Galatians were

early Christian believers, to whom a part of the Bible was written, and that of course they had long abandoned the flesh and minded only the things of the spirit. The epistle itself shows that they are wrong. St. Paul rebukes the Galatians most strongly for various faults which were undoubted marks of a fleshly mind. In the very verse before the text he had warned them against biting and devouring one another, and told them that they were in danger of being consumed one of another. And these are just the faults by which he showed the Corinthians to be carnal, that is, fleshly. "Ye are yet carnal," he writes to them, "for whereas there is among you envying, and strife, and divisions, are ye not carnal?" To these fleshly Galatians therefore he gives directions how they may escape fulfilling the lust of the flesh, as if there were no doubt about their wishing to escape it.

The strong language in which he rebukes them elsewhere shows that he cannot here be paying them mere idle compliments. It is just the same at the end of the next verse, where he tells them that because of the struggle going on between the spirit and the flesh "they could not do the things that they would"; and if we compare the text with the verses on the same subject in Romans, chap. vii., we can hardly doubt that by "the things which they would" he means "the good things which they would." This verse therefore likewise implies that they, the fleshly Galatians, did really wish to do good, but were prevented from doing good because their flesh struggled so hard against their spirit.

Some perhaps may think that, because St. Paul was a kind and charitable sort of man, he in words gave them credit for better thoughts, better wishes than they really had; that is, that he wrote thus only because he shrank from hurting their feelings. Certainly no man ever dealt out rebukes with more kindness and charity than St. Paul, but they are generally severe too; and at all events he never shows the least wish to make truth give way to charity, or to coax and flatter his converts into doing what he wished, by making them out to be any better than they really were.

St. Paul must then, it seems, have felt really sure that there was this better mind in the Galatians, and that they did wish not to fulfil the lust of the flesh. He saw among them abundant signs of a fleshly mind. Perhaps at the moment at which he wrote he saw signs of no mind except a fleshly mind. And yet he made bold to say that those signs told only half the truth, that under all the sins which called forth his anxious fears for their welfare there lurked a true and godly will to which he could still appeal as being indeed their very selves, and to which he could offer helpful advice.

We naturally ask why he had this confidence, why he regarded anything except the signs of fleshliness and sin, which indeed he could not disregard. The epistle itself partly suggests the answer. His most earnest warnings are founded on the remembrance of the signs of goodness which they had shown in former days. "Having begun in the Spirit," he asks, "are ye now made perfect by the flesh?"

P

"Now, after that ye have known God, or rather were
known of God, how turn ye again to the weak and
beggarly elements?" and in this same chapter, "Ye
did run well; who did hinder you that ye should not
obey the truth?" What they once had been he
could not doubt that they might become again. It
was but too plain that the good was now for the
time hidden and depressed by the foolish and wicked
counsels to which they had yielded when once the
first warmth of their early zeal had cooled off. Yet,
though hidden and depressed, it could not by that
time be destroyed; it lay there for the while motion-
less and helpless, yet able to answer to the call of a
voice from heaven coming through the Apostle whose
preaching had first brought them from darkness into
light.

It would be too much to suppose that St. Paul
knew personally every member of the Galatian
Church to which he was writing in this broad and
unshrinking way. Doubtless all that he said about
the Church at large he could have said with equal
truth about many of the men of whom the Church
was made up. But probably not of all. There must
have been some whose sins were now troubling him,
in whose case he had no happy recollection of former
devotion to encourage him in believing that its
sparks were still smouldering within their hearts.
Yet to them too—to one and all—he gives the same
counsel, and expects the same answering consent, in
heart if not in action.

Nor again was it by an idle kind of guess work
that St. Paul passed from those whom he knew to

those whom he did not know. For after all it was
not the mere remembrance of past blessedness that
was the only or the deepest ground of St. Paul's
confidence in his present appeal : that was an easily
handled outward ground, common to him and the
Galatians, which he could speak of and point to as
a thing not to be disputed by any one, a part of
their actual outward history. It was also to himself
a cheering picture, a help by which he might keep
his whole mind in entire reliance on the faith of his
inmost spirit, a token and pledge which pointed
unmistakeably to truths not only deeper but also
wider than itself.

And here the question about St. Paul becomes the
question about ourselves, whether we will or no.
What warrant has any one, what warrant, for instance,
have I, for using such language towards those whose
lives he has not personally known, as St. Paul had
known many of the Galatian converts ? Is it right
to use weaker and more guarded language until years
of acquaintance have made him familiar with the
personal history of his hearers ? If this were so, I
do not see how it would be possible for me to preach
to you from this place. I could not for years to
come say from personal knowledge of the facts
of your lives " Ye did run well : who did hinder
you that ye should not obey the truth ?" St. Paul's
example is therefore full of encouragement : the real
grounds of his hope came from another source than
what his eyes had seen or his ears heard : and from
that same source a like hope may rightly spring
even now, even from the nature of man and of every

man, and from the work which God is ever carrying
on within every man.

St. Paul knew that man was created by God in
His own image, to obey Him and to love Him: that,
when man obeyed God and loved Him, he was not
adding some new thing to his nature, but was fulfilling his nature : that, when he disobeyed and hated
God, he was doing as unnatural a thing, and standing
in as wrong and perverted a manner, as if a tree were
set with its branches in the earth and its roots
pointing to the sky : hence, though sin bent and
wrenched him out of the right way, that he still had a
spring within him ever tending to bring him back to
his right state. And if that was true even of heathens,
how much more of those to whom God was fully made
known in His Son Jesus ! The dim vague feeling
after One whom they scarcely knew and whom something within them struggled to obey, they knew not
why, had been exchanged for faith in the Son of God
who had come from heaven to draw all men up to
Himself, and so to the Father who had sent Him :
and thus they had learned that those dim notions
which they could not understand were indeed the
yearnings of children for a loving Father from whom
they had long been estranged, but apart from whom
and in rebellion from whom they were at variance
with their true selves. This new faith had not conquered the old enemy who had led them astray into
disobedience and hatred. He still had for a while
great power over their hearts. It was still only by
hard and determined striving that they could keep
their true place nigh to God and in subjection to His

will.   Only they now knew how it was not a mere
unknown voice within them, but their truest and best
selves, which would answer Amen to St. Paul or any
other who declared that they desired not to fulfil the
will of the flesh.

The same ground of hope belongs to every
Christian preacher still, if he will.   He need not wait
for outward signs to assure him that his people's
hearts are sometimes turned to God, delightful and
useful as such signs may be to give life and substance
to a faith which may easily become shadowy and
thin.   It is enough for him that they are stamped
with Christ's mark, and temples of the Holy Ghost.
Nor is it for preachers only that this confidence is
provided.   Every one who has a conscience has
many a time to preach to himself short and sharp
little week-day sermons.   Yet sharp and sincere as
they may be, they will have little lasting power,
unless he can see clearly, and believe strongly that,
bad as he may be, he has a better mind of his own,
and can feel that in fighting God's battle within himself he is in fact fighting his own battle.

And yet who among us can say that to escape
from fulfilling the lust of the flesh is the chief or
habitual desire of his heart?   Yet only so far as that
is our desire can St. Paul's counsel be of any use to
us.   If we are willing to fulfil the lust of the flesh, of
what use can it be to us to be told how to avoid fulfilling it?   The word "lust" here, as in most passages
of the Bible, means much more than it generally
means in the present day : it means desires or
covetings of all kinds: the lust of the flesh is nothing

more nor less than the desire of the flesh. So too
the word "flesh" does not here mean either sin
generally, or simply our bodies : it is all the lower
part of our nature, especially therefore our bodies, so
far and only só far as it sets itself up against the
higher part of our nature and strives to have a
will of its own. We men, made of the dust of the
ground and yet breathed into by the Spirit of God,
are on the one side a part of the outward and
visible world, and on the other akin to God Himself.
Like animals our bodies are born, and grow, and are
nourished by food, and give birth to others of our
race, and fall sick and die, and our dust returns to
the ground from which it was first made. But that
which in animals is their whole self in us is only the
lower part of ourself, not our truest self at all. That
in us which cannot be seen or heard or felt, which is
fed not with meat or drink but with knowledge and
love, that is, our spirit, is our truest self.

But in our present state the body and all the
wonderful powers which connect it with the spirit
have been ever striving to break away from obedience
to the spirit, and to set up for themselves as a separate being, that is, as an animal. Now one thing
which mainly strikes us about animals is that, whatever they do, they seem to do because they cannot
help it. They have no power of choice between this
thing or that. Most of their actions come to them
not by being taught, or by seeing that it is wise and
right to do them, but because it is, as we say, their
nature. In others they merely obey their desires
whenever they are felt. If two desires clash, and

they do not yield to one, it is because it draws them less feebly, not because they reject it. And this is the state to which we too should come, if our flesh could wholly fulfil its desire.

There are few of us, I fear, who have not, strange to think, actually sometimes longed that such were our state, longed to have nothing to do but to fill ourselves with abundance of eating and drinking and sleeping and every other animal enjoyment. But that dream cannot last undisturbed, when once a single thought of parents or children or brothers and sisters or God has broken in. It may have sad power of us still, but it cannot keep us wholly for its own.

On some future day I hope to consider the sovereign remedy of which St. Paul has told us in the opening words of the text. Meanwhile for to-day let us take to ourselves the help which the next verse holds out to us, if we have made up our minds that, so far as in us lies, we will not fulfil the desire of our flesh. Let us at least meet the desire of the flesh with a deeper and stronger desire of the spirit. If we, our true selves, cannot have complete possession, at least let us not yield the field. Let us first maintain the battle with the rebellious flesh, that at last victory may be ours. For without doubt, brethren, so it may be, if we will. Let us hold fast our faith, hope, and love. The victory will come at last. Death, the last enemy, shall be destroyed when this corruptible shall have put on incorruption, and this mortal shall have put on immortality. Let us think on those shouts of our future triumph, O death, where is thy sting? O grave, where is thy victory? But while we are still fighting, yet other words are put into our lips, "Have mercy upon me, O Lord, for I am weak: O Lord, heal me, for my bones are vexed. My soul also is sore vexed: but thou, O Lord, how long?" And when we ask "How long?" God's answer is, till we have tried and proved His succour. If He always came to our succour at once, we might not feel the struggle; and then we might boast of our own strength, and through that boasting never come to victory. We are indeed told, "Thou shalt cry," and the Lord shall say, "Here I am." Yet sometimes God is most truly with us when He delays His aid, and He is with us by that very delay: for, if He made haste to accomplish His will all at once, it might be that the work of healing in us might not be perfected. Let us still cry to Him without ceasing, believing that He knows best how to help us; and then we shall hear Him saying to us as He said to St. Paul, "My grace is sufficient for thee; for my strength is made perfect in weakness."

XXI

THE BATTLE OF SPIRIT AND FLESH, AND THE LIFE IN THE SPIRIT

St. Ippolyts, Fifteenth Sunday after Trinity, 1857.

II

"I SAY then, Walk in the Spirit, and ye shall not fulfil the lust of the flesh. For the flesh lusteth against the spirit, and the spirit against the flesh : and these are contrary the one to the other: so that ye cannot do the things that ye would."—*Gal.* v. 16, 17.

ON Sunday last I tried to bring before you part of the meaning of these verses, and especially of the 16th verse. I pointed out that, when St. Paul said to the Galatians, " Walk in the Spirit, and ye shall not fulfil the lust of the flesh," he must have believed that in some way or other the Galatians wished not to fulfil the lust of the flesh, and therefore would be glad to learn how they might avoid fulfilling it : that they were indeed, as St. Paul's own language shows, fleshly enough in their acts, but still that their truest and inmost selves desired not to fulfil the desire of the flesh. I said that St. Paul's faith in

this better mind of the Galatians sprung partly from
the faith and spirituality which he had himself
formerly seen in some of them, but still more from
the knowledge that they were all men created in the
image of God Himself, redeemed with the blood of
His Son, and worked upon by His Holy Spirit
within them : and further that all Christian preachers
have a right, in thinking of and speaking to their own
congregations, to act upon the faith which encouraged
St. Paul when he was writing to the Galatians, since
we too are born of the same family, and baptized
into the same Church as they were.   Further, I tried
to show you that the lust of the flesh means the
desire of the flesh, that is, the desire of our body and
the powers which belong to the body, so far as they
set themselves up as separate from our spirit and
against our spirit ; that therefore to fulfil the desire
of the flesh means to act just as if we were mere
animals, as if we had no spirits to keep our bodies in
order and teach them what they should do.   Lastly
I said that if we really wished not to fulfil the lust or
desire of the flesh, we might at least fight against it
by means of the lust or desire of the spirit, which we
have within us too, as the 17th verse tells us ; and I
promised to speak another time of that walking in
the Spirit which St. Paul recommends in the 16th
verse.   Before doing this however I wish to say a
few more words about the 17th verse.   Although it
very rightly comes after the 16th, it in one respect
comes before it as to the sense, for it contains the
reason which St. Paul gives for using the language
with which the text begins.   The higher and more

difficult thought of walking in the spirit as a means of not fulfilling the desire of the flesh is partly explained by the better known struggle between the flesh and the spirit. "For the flesh lusteth, or desireth," he says, "against the spirit, and the spirit against the flesh, and these are contrary the one to the other." This also is an appeal to something within the knowledge and conscience of the Galatians : but it is different from the appeal in the former verse. St. Paul does not here say which is the better, the spirit or the flesh, or which best spoke on behalf of the true self of each single Galatian. He only calls attention to the wrestling which he knew, and which they could not help knowing, if they thought a little about the matter, was going on within them. Who is there that has not felt such wrestlings ? Who has not felt himself going two ways at once, desiring to do some pleasant but wrong thing, and desiring to abstain from the wrong thing however pleasant it might be ? The wrestlings might end in different ways. The one or the other wrestler might be thrown. The flesh or the spirit might be the winner. That is not what St. Paul is here speaking of, but of the struggle itself. When the flesh desires against the spirit, the spirit cannot help desiring against the flesh, if it does not lie wholly asleep. And why is this ? Because they are contrary the one to the other. They cannot be separate without being at war. The flesh is intended to act always as the servant of the spirit: and when it tries to act by itself and for itself, it cannot merely leave the spirit alone ; it must act against the spirit. And the spirit must also act against this rebellious flesh, unless it has been beaten down into insensibility by being often conquered. This is not a doctrine that we are expected to believe because the Bible tells us so, as if we should know nothing of the kind by ourselves. The Bible only reminds us of what we know but too well already. Because the battle is going on and must go on between the desires of the flesh and the spirit, therefore it is that the Bible takes up the matter, and tells us how to deal with it. It is certainly worth our while to have a clear short account of our condition given, as we have it given to us here ; but after all that would be poor comfort, if the Bible did not tell us how to mend our condition. But first we must boldly face the worst. It will not do to go on in a lazy way, dimly conscious of thoughts and desires jostling each other within us, but never asking ourselves which are right and which wrong, which we are yielding to and which we are thrusting away from us. God calls upon us to look within. Can it be that we know of no such struggle within us ? If there is no resistance of one thing against another, it is full time to ask ourselves to which desire we have wholly yielded. Surely we must feel at times desires of the flesh rising up within us. If then no desire of the spirit rises up also within us to fight with them, may it not unhappily be that we have wholly consented to the flesh ? War and strife are sad things, but a deadly and corrupting peace is far worse. It is better to be always at war within than to buy peace by letting the flesh have all its cravings. And what hope can we have that we shall ever be able to conquer, if we have not yet begun to fight?

But fighting implies an enemy. Is our own flesh then an enemy? Might not some of us answer that, if the strife is between two parts of himself, he has no wish that either should conquer? Our flesh is surely part of ourselves; why should we, how can we, treat part of ourselves as our enemy, even if it be the enemy of some part of us? Such thoughts are sure to occur to our own minds: if they did not, some one else would suggest them to us. Let us by all means look at them closely, and not shrink from them as altogether wicked. Nothing certainly could be more dreadful than to think of our flesh as some strange and foreign thing which we should wish to destroy. That is a false and blasphemous notion, though there are thousands of people all over the world, Christians, heathens, and infidels, who believe it. He who made our spirit made our flesh also. It cannot be His will that we should seek to destroy His work. But in truth it is not against the body that the spirit strives, but against the wilful and rebellious action of the body. We never find in the Bible the strong and harsh language respecting the flesh applied to the body itself. The striving and desiring of the spirit is not, I say, to destroy the body, but to overcome its deepset proneness to rebel and bring it into service to itself, as the order of God's creation required. For though He made the body, it was only to obey and serve the spirit that He made it, and all wayward action of its own is not of His making or appointing. We look forward to a time beyond the grave, when the body shall freely and joyfully obey the slightest wishes of the spirit without check and hindrance, and our work in this life must be to advance towards that heavenly state, and, as far as we can, to calm the disorder of the unruly flesh. Till that is accomplished the struggle must go on, not as though the spirit hated the flesh, but because the spirit loves the flesh, and therefore desires to bring it back to its true place and work.

The last words of the text describe the result of the struggle, "So that ye cannot do the things that ye would." This is St. Paul's account of our slavery, a slavery as true and complete as any to which negroes are subject. We call him a slave who cannot do the things that he wishes, who is obliged to do the things that his master wishes, and cannot escape from him. We call ourselves free here in England because we can in a measure do what we wish. But after all there are bounds to this freedom, bounds set by the presence and neighbourhood of our fellowmen, although they may be in no sense our masters ; bounds set by all the things around us, into which we are born, and out of which we never can wholly struggle away. But surely the narrowest bounds are within ourselves. When we have resolved to fulfil some desire, our better nature often says "No," and thus either keeps us from doing what we would, or vexes and haunts us while we are doing it, so as to keep us from enjoying it, and thus in either case we cannot really do the things that we would. Here it is the spirit that keeps the flesh from doing what it would, though we have been willing to go along with the flesh. But, as I said before, the text probably refers rather to the good things that we would, to the desires of the spirit which are hampered by the desires of the flesh. How many good resolutions have we not all of us made and really desired to fulfil, and yet been checked and hindered by the motions of our flesh, which shrank from pain and urged us on to pleasure! Sometimes we do not like to say that it was we that desired to do those good deeds ; we had rather say it was something in us, our spirit perhaps, as St. Paul says. Yes, truly, and yet St. Paul was right when he spoke of the things that *we* would. He knew better than we often know ourselves what is the true " we." Those good desires, he tells us, are ours ; they show forth that which God made us to be : let us only carry them out, and not suffer any part of us to rebel against the whole. What can be more humbling or wrong than that we should not be able to do the things that we would ?

But how can we escape this slavery and disgrace ? How can we get back our freedom, and have peace within ourselves ? " Walk in the Spirit," answers St. Paul, " and ye shall not fulfil the desire of the flesh." All our shameful helplessness comes from our being so willing to give way to the desire of the flesh. Let us once overcome that, and we shall enter upon peace and freedom ; and the way to overcome that is by walking in the Spirit. Observe, he does not say by fulfilling the desire of the spirit. That belongs to the strife of which he is going to speak in the next verse, a strife which is made necessary only by the rebellion of the flesh.   Although the flesh is so ready to trouble the spirit, the spirit is not at all ready to trouble the body, and would rather be at peace with it.

To walk in the Spirit is not therefore a restless and warlike thing.   It means that whatever we do we should do from spiritual motives, by spiritual means, in a spiritual manner.   We should move about in and breathe the things of the Spirit, just as our bodies move about in and breathe the air.   The Galatians desired to live almost entirely by outward customs and laws, neglecting the inward movements of the Spirit.   They made a great deal of circumcision, and wished to admit none as Christians, however truly they might believe in Christ, unless they submitted to the old Jewish law by cutting off a piece of flesh.   They set a great value on outward works, and cared very little for the inward spirit which breathed through the works.   In all this they were not walking in the Spirit.   Even when they did right actions, they were not walking in the Spirit, and therefore they were almost helpless to withstand the desires of the flesh.   Perhaps the meaning of this is not very clear, so that it may be well to explain it by an instance.   In the 15th verse St. Paul accuses them of biting and devouring one another.   This they did because they obeyed certain lusts of the flesh, vanity, or desire of importance, or desire of power, or even desire of money.   Suppose they came to learn how wrong it was to quarrel with each other in this dreadful manner, and to see that

the desires of the flesh were at the bottom of their
disorders, we can easily imagine that they would
resolve to quarrel no more, because quarrelling was
wrong. In this they would be perfectly right, and
yet I fear they would very often fail. They might
now and then succeed in keeping down some beginning of discord, but often enough they would fail
when their passions were strongly kindled. And no
wonder ; for though these efforts of theirs might be
quite right, they still would not be walking in the
Spirit : to walk in the Spirit in this matter would
be not merely to try not to quarrel, but actually
to love their neighbours truly and sincerely. If
only they did really love their neighbours, they would
not often need a hard struggle to keep from quarrelling with them. The flesh knows nothing at all
about love : the word means nothing to it : it knows
nothing about right or wrong : it only asks whether
a thing is pleasant or unpleasant. Love and right
and wrong belong to the spirit, and to the spirit
only. When they are the objects which we set
before us in all our thoughts, then we walk in the
Spirit, and all the striving in the world not to
do wrong actions will not help us much unless
we give full play to the deepest and inmost springs
of our spirit. We cannot keep our hands from evil
unless we fill our hearts with the desire of good.

Perhaps it may occur to us that this advice of St.
Paul may be very beautiful, but not very useful,
since it seems to offer to help us in a hard matter by
bidding us take refuge in a harder. To resist the
desires of the flesh may be no easy matter to poor,

Q

weak, suffering men; but what is that to walking in
the Spirit! So indeed we must think so long as we
look on walking in the Spirit as a mere matter of
striving and struggling. But the spirit of man lives
only by dwelling in the Spirit of God, and that is
not a matter of striving and struggling at all. We
may have struggling enough to keep back all the
powers of evil that would fain drag us down from
the life in the Spirit; but the life in the Spirit comes
to us only as the free gift of God, and we have but
to open our hearts to Him, and He will bestow it in
full measure. He is ever seeking to be with us in
all our doings, to be ever speaking to us, to be ever
showing Himself to us. He does not ask us to do
any great things to bring us into His presence. He
offers Himself freely to us, and entreats us not to
cast Him away from us. When we suffer Him to
be with us, then all the things of the spirit grow and
are strong within us, and we too have such a freedom
and strength as we hardly dreamed of before. The
unruly motions of the flesh may still remain; but the
battle with them is quite another thing from what
it was before. It is no longer a miserable quarrel
between two members of our nature, but a part of
the war which God is carrying on against all that
disturbs His wise creation. And if God be for us,
who can be against us?

In the last few days, dear brethren, God has
visited us to break the heavy chain of custom and
absence of change in which the strength of the
desire of the flesh chiefly lies. When sickness comes
among us, and the strength of our proud and wilful

flesh becomes weakness, He bids us take courage and carry the fight bravely on, if indeed we have begun it. When death itself lays any of us low, then the open grave and the words that are spoken over it preach more truly and plainly than any sermon can do the higher glory and power of the Spirit which shall quicken the body to a second life. Such times bring out whatever life of the spirit there is in any of us. They are opportunities, which it is grievous to neglect, for breaking off the dull bondage of sloth and hardness of heart. Whatever grief, or tenderness, or love, or faith is called out in any of us is a token that our spirits are not dead, and that the Spirit of God is calling upon us not to quench the holy fire which He has kindled, but to suffer it to burn on henceforth in the midst of health and common, unbroken life. And it is only in this life of the Spirit that we can still hold communion with those whose flesh has passed away into dust. If it is a comfort to friends in distant lands to look up to the blue sky and know that both are gazing at the same sun, how much greater comfort is it to be looking daily and nightly upon the face of the Father of spirits, and believe that they who are no longer with us in the body are still looking yet more fully on that same blessed face, and that, wherever they may be, they are in the hands of Him who gave His flesh for the life of the world.

XXII

[THE UNSPEAKABLE GIFT OF GOD]

Christchurch, Barnwell, Cambridge, Fifteenth Sunday after Trinity,
at a Harvest Festival, 1876.

"THANKS be unto God for his unspeakable gift."—2 *Cor.* ix. 15.

OUR service of to-day is a service of thanksgiving.
We are not accustomed to give the name thanksgiving to the services of the various Christian fes-
tivals which we celebrate as members of Christ's
Church, and which are laid down for us in our
Prayer Book; but though we do not use the name,
we are not the less engaged in thanksgiving in any
due observance of those hallowed days. They all,
in one way or another, bring before us the different
steps in the great work of enlightening and saving
mankind which God has already wrought in His Son
Jesus Christ. Their first and clearest use is to rouse
our hearts into thankfulness for the supreme blessings
from God's hands which we have inherited as heirs
of the kingdom.

But indeed no prayer, no worship can in strict

truth be called Christian which does not spring out
of thankfulness, and which, in spirit at least, if not
in words, is not mingled with thanksgiving.   A
Christian prayer is not a cry to an unknown Power
in the distance, but a trustful pleading of children
with a Father whom they have learned to know as
a Father indeed by the sending of His Son.   A
Christian prayer is no mere pursuit of good things
now in the keeping of One able and willing to let us
have them; it is full of the remembrance of His
well-tried love, and therefore in all that it seeks from
Him seeks yet more Himself.   For Christians a
thankless prayer is a godless prayer; and when they
come into His presence, their first thought must be
of the ever-new glad tidings how the way to His
presence was opened to them.   That familiar plan
on which our Collects have been written, of setting
forth some assurance of God's goodness before they
lead us to ask for anything to be given us, is a
simple example of thanksgiving as the foundation of
prayer; and from other parts of our services in
various shapes the same lesson may be learned.

But the greatest of all thanksgivings is that Holy
Communion in which many of us are about to join.
The meaning of the ancient name by which it is still
sometimes called, the Eucharist, is the thanksgiving;
and in that light we are taught to regard the Holy
Communion by the prayer in our own service in
which we "entirely desire God's fatherly goodness
mercifully to accept this our sacrifice of praise and
thanksgiving."   If only we kept this meaning of the
Holy Communion as a thanksgiving more clearly

and steadily before us, it would save us from many of the false beliefs and perverted feelings which haunt men's minds in the presence of God's holy table.   The sacrifice already completed, the gift of gifts already bestowed, the fellowship and communion with the heavenly Lord, and with things unseen, and with all God's redeemed children already established,—these would fill our hearts and leave no room for thoughts that drive God into the far distance in seeming to bring Him near.   In the spirit of thanksgiving, and in that spirit alone, can we renew the sacrifice of ourselves and of all that belongs to us to be living instruments of Christ's kingdom.

But the Holy Communion is not only a thanksgiving: it is also a harvest thanksgiving.   Each time that it is celebrated it carries within it a sense closely resembling the purpose of this our yearly service.   When it was instituted by our Lord Himself at the Last Supper, we are told in all the four accounts preserved for us in the New Testament that He " gave thanks"; and we may be sure that this striking fact was written down for our instruction.   The thanksgiving which our Lord pronounced was probably in the words used by the Jews at the Passover meal, blessings rendered to God the Creator of the corn and the vine.   At all events this must have been the subject of His thanksgiving.   The new act of communion which He was about to appoint for His disciples was to take its rise out of the actual supper of which they were partaking. It was already a religious meal ; but a meal still, a

meal which showed how God would have us regard
all our meals. And thus the thanksgiving for human
food under two great heads, the wine that maketh
glad the heart of man, and the bread that strengthens
man's heart,—a thanksgiving offered to the Maker of
heaven and earth, by whose wisdom and power the
living plants which give birth to the bread and the
wine are brought forth and nourished by the earth,
and brought to perfection by the rain and the sun,—
in this way, I say, the thanksgiving for ordinary food
was carried on into our high Christian festival.

In ancient times a part of the service itself had
very distinctly the same purpose.   Bread and wine
were solemnly offered to God with thanksgivings,
not only for the blessings of Christ's redemption, but
for the blessings of the earth's produce.   The offering
itself was an act of thanksgiving, a rendering back to
God of that which had been received from Him, as
the uttered praises were words of thanksgiving.   The
communion which followed was a joyful partaking of
God's gifts by men who met together as members of
one divine family, and rejoiced to mingle their whole
life, its earthliest necessities as well as its holiest
memories and hopes, with the worship of God their
Saviour.

Each time therefore that we meet before God's
table, we too shall do well to let the bread and wine
lead back our thoughts to the thanksgiving which
our Lord Himself pronounced over them, and lift up
our hearts to Him from whom all good things proceed.   Our proper harvest festival will thus find
echoes throughout the year, on each day of which

we are all receiving of its benefits ; and our Holy
Communions themselves may perchance be found to
gain a firmer hold upon all our lives.

We need not fear to go astray by joining earthly
and heavenly things together. Not this is dangerous ;
but rather to keep them apart from each other, either
in our own inward thoughts or in our prayers and
praises to the throne of grace. Earthly things are apt
to become as it were only earthy, heavenly things are
apt to become thin and shadowy, when we do not
suffer them to lead to each other, forgetting that,
whether we eat or drink or whatever we do, we may
either do all to the glory of God or to His dishonour.
He who knew what was in man taught us in the
same breath to say ' Hallowed be Thy Name,' and
' Give us this day our daily bread.'   The full sense
of each petition will become clearer to us according
as we learn to pray them both together.

This lesson of the Holy Communion is repeated
to us in another way by the words of St. Paul which
form the text. " Thanks be unto God for his unspeakable gift."   The gift of which St. Paul writes
here can be no other than the most precious and the
most utterly wonderful of gifts, the gift of God's only
begotten Son. And yet the course of his teaching
throughout the chapter, almost to these its last words,
has seemed to concern itself with much lower things.
He is speaking about a collection which some of the
Gentile Churches were proposing to make for the
distressed Christians of Judaea. He was anxious
that the Corinthians should not be behindhand in
fulfilling their promise ; that they should fulfil it

cheerfully as men rejoicing to bless as God blesses, using what they had received from Him as a means of multiplying His benefits. The Corinthian bounty, which to those who looked on the outward surface might seem to be only a means of feeding starving bodies, St. Paul saw to carry with it a power of spiritual enrichment, creating fresh bonds of loving interest on the part of the givers and fresh bonds of loving gratitude on the part of the receivers, with thanksgivings rising to God the first Giver from the hearts of all, both for the food which He had enabled to be given and received, and for the sense of brotherly fellowship which had been kindled by the giving and receiving. He recalls what Isaiah had said about the manifoldly fruitful power of every word that comes forth from God, as an act of His providence, bread-corn and seed at once, satisfying hunger and bearing fresh growths of fruit ; not returning to Him void, but accomplishing that which He pleased, and prospering in all whereunto He sent it. Thus all St. Paul's expectations of results to follow from the Gentile gifts lead him back to the exceeding grace of God, of which they and their fruits were but parts—and yet true examples, showing the manner in which God's exceeding grace works. And so he closes all that he has to say on what some would call this small practical matter with a thanksgiving from his own heart and lips for that one signal gift of God's grace, in the light of which alone can any of His other gifts be rightly understood.

He calls it an unspeakable gift, a gift which cannot be told out and expounded and set forth to the utter-

most.   This means much more than saying that it is
a very great gift indeed, or a very precious gift indeed.
It means that we may go on telling out the various
things that are contained in it, and yet never come
to the end of them.   When God gave us His Son,
gave Him up to suffer death for our sakes, gave Him
raised again from the dead, it was no single benefit
that He bestowed, but an infinite and ever-flowing
fountain of benefit.   In proportion as we understand
that first gift,—and we never can understand it except
so far as we ourselves enter into the mind of Christ,—
we shall recognize gifts on every side where hitherto
our blinded eyes have seen nothing but emptiness or
even injuries, and if the gifts thus seen are rightly and
thankfully used, we shall find them multiplying and
leading on to gifts as yet unseen.

Our Lord has bid us look upon the birds of the
air, and consider how our heavenly Father feeds
them, and then He has asked, "Are ye not much
better than they?"   This saying of His goes beyond
its immediate lesson of trust.   The two words "Father"
and "heavenly" would alone suffice to mark the difference between the feeding of birds and the feeding of
men.   For us, for even the most thoughtless of us,
those two words have a meaning which colours every
part of our lives, even the lowest.   For us men,
Christian men, a harvest thanksgiving ought not to
be simply a thanksgiving for the means of satisfying
a natural and necessary hunger, such as the hunger of
the birds.   The food which God gives is given to
sustain us in the doing of His work.   In receiving
it as from Him, we acknowledge Him as the true

Master of our doings, whom we are either serving faithfully, or undutifully disregarding in all to which we set our hand. And this service of ours is not the service of slaves but of children, to whom it has been given to know and to be blessed by His love. Thus in giving Him sincere and willing thanks for His gift of the earth's produce, we have our feet on the lowest step of a ladder which leads up to the cross of Christ.

Let us then gladly seize this occasion of rejoicing with the pure and life-giving joy of thankfulness on behalf of ourselves and our brethren. Let us welcome a festival which brings God before us as caring for the simplest wants of His creatures. It is our own fault if we stop there, and cast out of remembrance the deeper wants which He yet more wonderfully supplies. If we join humbly and sincerely in the services of to-day, we shall be on the way towards learning to read all His dealings in the light of the one unspeakable gift which is above all and which includes all.

XXIII

THE EVANGELIST A PHYSICIAN

Great Saint Mary's Church, before the University, St. Luke's Day, 1864.

"To give light to them that sit in darkness and in the shadow of death, to guide our feet into the way of peace." —*Luke* i. 79.

THE knowledge which the Church possesses of St. Luke, so far as it is of any wide and lasting interest, is comprised in three facts, that he was a physician, that he was the faithful companion of St. Paul, and that he was the author of our third Gospel and the Acts of the Apostles. In one or more of these characters alone can we summon up his image, when we desire to commemorate with gratitude and honour his share in the work of building up the Apostolic Church. The distinctive lineaments of some among St. Luke's fellow-labourers cannot now be seized with any force or clearness : in his case the fault is our own if his name leaves only a vague impression behind.

And in this place there is less excuse than elsewhere for looking on the periodical honouring of apostles and evangelists as an artificial arrangement, too venerable indeed to disturb, yet not answering to any present needs. In our annual commemorations of those who in various times have rendered services to our academical body, we have a useful help towards remembering that the familiar names of our Church Calendar are the names of benefactors too; benefactors not merely to a single local corporation but to the One Universal Church ; yet not the less truly benefactors to ourselves, all as having helped to build the foundation on which we rest and likewise build, some yet more, as speaking directly to us, across the ages, their messages of holy wisdom. Our sense of true obligation may be quickened yet more by the culture which here finds an appropriate home. The advancing study of history is barren of reverence and humility for none but those who bring to it no reverence or humility themselves. To learn with increasing conviction the infinite variety and com- plication of all human doings, and at the same time to discern here and there among them the traces of laws overwhelming in their vastness, is a discipline that may seem to weak brains and cold hearts to justify them in refusing to honour the men of old time, even as in ignoring the Eternal Ruler of whose will they all were ministers. But such crude misuse of God's latest gifts should find no place with us who possess so abundantly His earlier gifts. With us every new aspect of history comes in to enrich and expand the old, not to supersede them. The same thoughtful research, which discloses the wide influence of general causes, sometimes of a physical nature,

over the actions of men, brings out with equal vividness the marvellous power of individual energy and
character.   The same patient and truthful study of
thought and language, which has shown how wide a
difference between ourselves and the men of old time
may be concealed by identity of words, has revealed
a yet deeper community in the more vital parts of our
nature, and thus pointed out how ancestral experience
may most effectually be used for our guidance in the
mazes of the later world.   Such advantages have we
for cultivating a simple and intelligent affection for
the first heralds of the Word of Life.

On the other hand we must rest satisfied without
a detailed biography.   In this respect St. Luke holds
an intermediate position.   Just enough is recorded to
save him from being to us no more than a bodiless
voice.   It is pleasant to think of the support which
his staunch devotedness gave to St. Paul in the hour
of extreme trial.   That last act of generous courage
worthily crowns the personal interest inspired by his
share in the journeyings of the great Apostle.   But
of his own individual labours among mankind and
their results we know, it may be said, absolutely
nothing.   His two books are the abiding legacy
which manifestly claims our gratitude, and from
which almost alone we must gather the materials
for such idea as we may be able to frame of his
likeness.   It is chiefly in this connection that his
occupation as a physician and his relation to St.
Paul deserve to be constantly remembered.

The significance of St. Luke's profession may be
variously interpreted.   The Collect for to-day is

founded on a broad ideal ground. We pray Him
who called Luke the physician to be an evangelist
and physician of the soul, that by the wholesome
medicines of the doctrines delivered by him all the
diseases of our souls may be healed. In accordance
with the frequent practice of the Gospels, the earthly
work is taken as a figure of the diviner work, even as
Christ Himself bid St. Peter and St. Andrew leave
their boats to become fishers of men. Here however
the resemblance is yet nearer and more complete.
The diseases of the soul and those of the body are
connected by more than identity of name or partial
likeness. The idea of sin as a disease is not borrowed
from a passing phrase of Scripture, but expresses its
inmost mind as well as its habitual language. Nor is
this a matter of light consequence. This aspect of
sin, never perhaps formally denied, is rarely acknowledged in all its force. The sanction which it thus
receives, by being bound up with the Church's commemoration of St. Luke, is too weighty to be passed
by in silence.

Again, we might seek an historical connection
between the two kinds of labour in which we know
St. Luke to have been engaged. It is hardly worth
while to dwell on the minute exactness which some
have supposed to be discoverable where he has
occasion to notice the symptoms of disease. A more
difficult but a far more interesting task would be to
trace, if possible, in the Gospel and the Acts of the
Apostles that type of character and those habits of
thought which the practice of medicine would naturally engender in a mind too serious and impressible

not to be affected by its own pursuits. The one and
the self-same Spirit, dividing to every man severally as
he would, assuredly assigned to each labourer in the
Apostolic Church his special task of kindling and
enlightening the hearts of men according to the fitness of his past life ; and that noble, and in a true
sense of the word divine employment of healing men's
bodies was manifestly a preparation of peculiar value
for many offices in the service of the gospel. Thus
we cannot be wrong in assuming that there was a
divinely ordained sequence from Luke the physician
to Luke the evangelist. But it would be rash to lay
stress, with any pretensions to certainty, on the
evidence which we possess, as sufficient to prove that
the historical fact corresponded with the ideal truth.
Thus much only may be said without overloading the
Scriptural record with questionable ingenuities. Some
leading qualities of the mind disclosed to us in the
Gospel of St. Luke, and to a certain extent in the
Acts of the Apostles, are a gentle and tender
sympathy with all human suffering, a peculiar venera-
tion for all that can soothe or relieve it, and an
inclination to think of sinners chiefly as afflicted with
the worst and deadliest kind and cause of suffering.
These habits of mind are not confined to any one
class of men ; but at least they are the natural fruit
of that familiarity with sickness and pain, which,
despite the vulgar prejudice to the contrary, is
hardening only to those who are hard already. Thus
the doctrine which our Collect links to the name of
St. Luke would seem to have been in fact fulfilled in
himself. Not only was he at once physician and

evangelist, but his special work as an evangelist was to be the physician of sin-sick souls, and to represent to the end of time the precious truth so often lost among the barren abstractions of the theological intellect, that our Lord's most cherished title of Saviour, that which includes all that He has done for us men and for our salvation, means first and last that He is Christ the Healer.

St. Luke's personal attachment to St. Paul may be regarded, and has in fact been regarded, in two different lights as affecting his own writings. In the second century, when the Church found herself endowed, she scarcely knew how, with four distinct embodiments of the one everlasting gospel, it was naturally a cause of embarrassment that two out of the four carried in their titles no sanction of an Apostle's name. St. Mark and St. Luke had however been intimately associated with two of the most illustrious Apostles, and their authority was borrowed as in a manner extending to the works of the disciples. In St. Mark's case an express tradition deduced the written Gospel from the oral teaching of St. Peter. But history supplied no such warrant for St. Luke's narrative, and the defect was supplied by imagined allusions in St. Paul's epistles. Later students have hesitated to recognize that the third Gospel either needs or possesses any secondary guarantee of this nature from the latest born of the Apostles. Coincidences once thought to be decisive have ceased to carry weight. The concentration of St. Paul's whole heart and mind upon our Lord's death, resurrection

R

and ascension, as manifested to us in his own writings, is felt to throw grave doubt on the supposition that he would occupy himself to any great extent with the words and deeds of Christ's preceding ministry, either in his preaching to the people at large, or in his communings with a favoured friend and disciple. St. Luke himself will doubtless be more and more acknowledged as the sole author of the Gospel that bears his name, so far as that title to honour can be assigned to any one man.

But while the external bond of authority which connected St. Paul with St. Luke's Gospel has been loosening, a deeper and truer relationship has been discerned with increasing clearness. Few things have done so much to prepare the way for a restoration of the Bible to its former power over the hearts and minds of men, as the discovery of distinct types of doctrine as well as character among the Apostles themselves. Inconsistent as this state of things may be with the crude fancies which we are apt to indulge as to the form that a divine revelation ought to take, it is in perfect harmony with all that we know, on other grounds, of God's way of making Himself known to His creatures. Nay, we may perhaps find that the recognition of the fact is both a powerful and a timely help for keeping alive the faith in the possibility of revelation. The extravagant lengths to which the differences of the Apostles have been imagined to extend form no ground for refusing to see the variety which actually existed. It was necessary to outrage the best established rules of evidence, by which matters of literature and history are judged, before the ancient chieftains of our faith could be robbed of the dutifulness and reverence which are justly owing to them.

First among the variations of the Apostolic age stands the opposition between St. Paul and the Apostles of the circumcision, as disclosed to us in the Epistle to the Galatians. This is not the place to investigate the nature of that opposition, or to point out the limits—the narrow limits—within which it was confined. But in the background there lay a wide field of thought and feeling on which the lights and shadows struck with very different effect for the one side and for the other. Each aspect was compatible with a true vision of the Lord Jesus and His heavenly kingdom. The loss of either would have resulted for us in a fatal mutilation of the truth by which we live. But the difference was undeniably there, and to all appearance multitudes were affected by it.

St. Luke's peculiar intimacy with St. Paul leaves no doubt as to the side with which he would be ranged, if he belonged to either side at all. It is morally certain that the chosen companion of the foremost missionary to the Gentiles would look on Jew and Gentile respectively with the same eyes as his Master. We might further expect, though with less confidence, that these characteristics would be reflected in his writings. Whether this is indeed the case is not so obvious as to be entirely beyond dispute. Yet there is much in both the books which seems best accounted for by the ascendancy of St. Paul's thoughts.

Passing over details, we may observe with thankfulness that the task of writing the first and the representative history of the Church was committed to one for whom Jerusalem had ceased to be the central point of Christendom ; and whose hearty respect for the office and for the labours of the original Apostles in the first foundation of the Church, only enabled him to see more distinctly that the supreme controul of the illimitable future was entrusted to other hands. Even as on the Jewish side St. Peter was beyond all doubt a bond of union between the two divergent schools, so it is perhaps not too fanciful to think that St. Luke occupied a corresponding place among Gentile Christians. The perverse criticism, which assigns his writings to the next century, sees in them an effort to soften away differences, and help towards a reconciliation of the opposing camps. We who deny that any reconciliation was needed where there was neither war nor enmity, may nevertheless recognize, or think we recognize, some indications of a kindred temper, of a desire to quench the narrow-minded contempt which Gentiles no less than Jews were prone to indulge, and to vindicate the true position of Israel within the Church as well as before the Church, without for a moment relinquishing the broad Catholic ground which St. Paul had conquered with so much difficulty.

The same spirit acting under another form was apparently at work in the composition of St. Luke's Gospel, though the evidence there is certainly open to cavil. There is no such prominence given to

words and acts of the Lord favourable to the Gentile
cause, as has sometimes been imagined, nor is there
any keeping back of incidents which mark Him out
as a true child of Abraham according to the flesh.
On the other hand, far sterner sayings against the
Jews and prophecies of their doom than any recorded
in his Gospel may be gathered out of St. Matthew
and St. John. But this need not surprise us, if
we have a right understanding of his purpose.
Nothing could be less to his mind than to write
a controversial treatise under the guise of a history.
To all appearance he had no wish to make out a
case against the Jews for the sake of restraining
Judaism within the Church. His own heart was
filled with a calm conviction that the promise was
indeed to all whom the Lord God should call, and
this restful belief, freed from all antagonisms, seems
to shine through many of his words. He suffers the
opposition of Jew and Gentile to fall back as far as
was possible for a faithful witness of that Lord who
had often to pronounce open judgments on unbelieving
Israel. In its place we have the undivided humanity
inherited by Him who was the son of Adam as well
as the Son of David. Local Palestinian distinctions
are superseded by others of kindred import common
to all nations. St. Paul's idea of a universal Messiah,
the fulfilled hope of all the ends of the earth, seems
to be echoed in the story of St. Luke. Towards the
Jews themselves his tone is chiefly one of sorrowful
pity. Christ's weeping over Jerusalem, which he
alone relates, expresses with perfect truth the domi-
nant thought which this Gospel taken by itself would

suggest.   The vehement reproach of St. Paul, " Who
both killed the Lord Jesus and their own prophets,
and have persecuted us, and please not God, and are
contrary to all men":—such awful parables as · St.
Matthew records of the Two Sons, the Ten Virgins,
or the Sheep and the Goats;—such measured sen-
tences of solemn condemnation as St. John repeats,
and reiterates in his own person, are but faintly
represented here.   The words from the cross,
" Father forgive them, for they know not what
they do," whether transmitted by St. Luke's own
hand or by that of another, are an entirely faithful
exponent of his own mind, and of that side of our
Lord's person on which he most loved to dwell.
The true physician is there within the evangelist.
The guilt of those who crucified their King is
confessed to be not unmixed guilt, but also an
ignorance, a disease of the soul, the miserable result
of a chain of causes for which they were themselves
only in part responsible.   This is not perhaps the
language in which St. Paul would have chosen
to express his own thoughts : but it is such as a
love like his, which made him wish that he were
accursed from Christ for his brethren, his kinsmen
according to the flesh, might easily call forth in a
softer and less passionate spirit than his own.   It is
consistent with the most resolute determination not
to hamper the expanding Church with any Jewish
restraints that could injure its universality.

Such in rude outline are the influences which seem
to have determined the character of St. Luke as an
evangelist; the special apprenticeship of his pro-

fession and the special faith of his great Master in
the Gospel meeting together, and mingling with the
natural bent of his disposition. Let us now turn to
consider the words of the text for their own sake,
without asking too minutely what evidence may be
extracted from them as to the mental history of him
who has preserved them for our use. Those three
hymns, which we find in St. Luke alone, are remark-
able for the middle place which they hold between
Jewish and Christian devotion. The great prophets,
in whom the vision of future glory and restoration
had been brightest, supply glowing words which
raise yet higher the strain of ancient psalms. But
the one pervading thought which rules all others, if
thought it may be called, is a deep tranquil sense of
suspense ended, of longings satisfied, of hopes fulfilled. If we are surprised to find the joy itself so
nearly complete at a time when as yet the cycle of
gospel events was but beginning to run, this too has
a consolation of its own. Do we feel that we are
more ready to lift these or other like songs of grateful praise, because Christ has lived and died and
risen, and the Holy Ghost has descended, and all
that mighty plan has been accomplished? Do we
not enter with truer experience into that appealing
complaint of the prophet, where he bewails that all
the bitter and protracted birth-pangs of the Church
have only ended in wind, that no deliverance has
been wrought in the earth, neither have the inhabitants
of the world fallen? In his case the consciousness
of barrenness and failure never sinks into despair.
The unfailing stay of his soul, upon which he falls

back when every outward ground of confidence dis-
solves away, lies in the thought, "Trust ye in the
Lord for ever; for in the Lord Jehovah is everlasting
strength." The fountain of hope within him could never
be wholly dried up, for it was fed from a source
deep down below the upper world, where mutability
and misery and folly and sin seemed only too likely
to prevail. But however surely sustained by a living
faith, it was only a hope still, a hope that did not see
its own accomplishment. The hymns in St. Luke,
calmer in their outward expression, rejoice because
expectation has ended and fulfilment begun. But
such a rejoicing at such a season was possible only
because faith was as strong in Mary and Zacharias
and Simeon as it had been in Isaiah. In all the
deeds of homage which Scripture records as sur-
rounding the Infancy the same act of faith is repeated
—in the adoration of the Magi, in the joyful worship
of the shepherds. Vague as the thoughts of all
might be as to the nature of the coming deliverance,
none were staggered by the seeming disproportion
between its appearance and the encompassing realm
of darkness. The birth in the manger at Bethlehem,
in all its naked lowliness, might well have been
thought a strange power to oppose to the daily
pressure of a disordered world. All the misery and
confusion which weighed down the land of Israel in
the days of Herod the king was still there. No
hand was stretched out to restrain domestic oppressors
or foreign, Pharisees, publicans, or soldiers. No
check was seen to the advancing dissolution of
Israel's hereditary faith. A brazen firmament of

cruel tradition was fast overspreading the whole heaven, and threatened soon to blot out altogether the vision of Him who had once been known as a Father and a Redeemer. Yet still the confident songs went forth. "Blessed be the Lord God of Israel, for he hath visited and redeemed his people." "He hath put down the mighty from their seats, and exalted them of low degree. He hath filled the hungry with good things; and the rich he hath sent empty away." "Mine eyes have seen thy salvation, which thou hast prepared before the face of all people." If that faith was right and wise then, could it be out of place now? If the world seems to be dying once more, shall we do well to despair of the only true seed of life?

Between the primitive hymns and ourselves lies the whole history of Christendom. In its earlier stages the outward contrast between triumphant language and maimed accomplishment was repeated in various forms. At length a time came when it might be said with a certain truth that the grain of mustard seed had grown and waxed a great tree, and the nations of the earth were lodging in the branches of it. That time passed away, as indeed for many reasons it was needful that it should. But the later centuries have not brought a corresponding growth; must we not say that, here and there at least, they have brought decay? And so it is only too easy to fall into despairing thoughts, to persuade ourselves that the trial and the failure shut us out from the joyful belief which was possible while all was yet new. The true answer may be read in the letter and the spirit of these very hymns. Their apparent vagueness proceeds from their integrity of truth. The trust is in the Lord and His Anointed, not in any order of worship of Him, or compacted body of beliefs about Him, or forms of society and government built upon the acknowledgment of Him, such as existed around them by God's own appointment. All these might be necessary and divine. God is nothing to man if He is not worshipped; He cannot be worshipped without definite beliefs, His worship must be a ruling power in all man's doings; and without fixity and order in these things there is no abiding life. Nevertheless these things were made for man, not man for them; and that which should have been for his wealth too often becomes an occasion of falling. Other foundation can no man lay than that which is laid, which is Jesus Christ. But many buildings not wholly unworthy of the foundation may be laboriously built upon it, yet fail at last in the trial by fire; while, unscathed through all their failures, the foundation itself stands secure, the true object of primitive faith.

It is impossible to read these hymns without feeling how completely they harmonize with the image of. Christ the Saviour which is presented to us distinctively in St. Luke's Gospel, and perhaps it is not too much to say that the words of the text convey singly those traits in that divine form which moved him with the greatest power. He sets in the front of Christ's ministry, as if it best expressed to his mind the purpose of the whole, that announcement of His Mission in the words of Isaiah, " The

Spirit of the Lord is upon me, because he hath anointed me to preach the gospel to the poor ; he hath sent me to preach deliverance to the captives, and recovering of sight to the blind, to set at liberty them that are bruised, to preach the acceptable year of the Lord." In the same strain here is Zacharias rejoicing because " The dayspring from on high hath visited us, to give light to them that sit in darkness and in the shadow of death, to guide our feet into the way of peace." The music of the words need not hide the fulness and exactness of their meaning. Under two or three simple images is summed up the state of Israel at the hour when Christ came. And they are equally true now to describe the wants which His revelation can supply, the helpless confusion in which relief is despaired of, because it has been sought so often and not found. Darkness, the shadow of death, war ; these are the spells which the great Deliverer is pledged to break. Some may hesitate to accept a teaching which merges in these broad and sweeping forms the endless multiplicity of evil. There would be reason in the doubt, if we expected the outward face of the world to be changed in a moment as by a miracle. But the immediate freedom promised to us is not from the ills of life themselves, but from their curse, their sting, their power to vex and bind our spirits. This inward kingdom of evil can never be overthrown in detail. The first step towards destroying it is to realize its essential unity, even as it is most truly imaged in the figures of the Old Testament and of Zacharias. Innumerable evils, such even as may be and must be

for other purposes classed widely apart, sins and misfortunes and those evils which are both at once, are
all brought together with consummate truthfulness as
blinding our eyes and shutting us up in darkness, as
chilling us with the awful shadow of death, as dis-
tracting us within ourselves, and embroiling us with
our fellowmen in a trackless maze of warfare.   Deliverance begins when we attain a clear belief that
He who was welcomed as the dayspring from on
high is ready to meet us simply as the Lord of light
and life, the giver of peace, and the way to it ; and
when we read the book of His words and deeds in
the spirit of that assurance.   Other aspects of truth
remain behind to be laid hold of in due season.   But
none can take precedence of this.   That which brings
not good tidings has no power to heal.   The physician and the evangelist are eternally one.

XXIV

ALL THINGS OF, THROUGH, AND TO GOD

Emmanuel College Chapel, Last Sunday after Trinity, 1875.

" FOR of him and through him and to him are all things: to whom be glory for ever. Amen."—*Rom.* xi. 36.

ON ordinary Sundays it is natural and right that I should speak to you on lesser matters. Religious truth is made up of many doctrines : a holy and upright and kindly life is made up of many duties. They cannot all be spoken about at once. They must take their turn in our thoughts, now one coming specially before us, now another. But to-day I would rather ask you to consider this one great all-embracing subject on which all the others depend. The mighty faith of St. Paul, in which he wrote these memorable words, is what we shall require to carry with us at all times, whenever we desire light from heaven to fall upon any one of our earthly ways.

We need not linger long on the train of thoughts in St. Paul's mind which found their ending in the

text, but we must look at them for a few moments
that we may understand the text better. His heart
was filled with sorrow because so many of the Jews
rejected our Lord. It was a great comfort and joy
to him that so many Gentiles had embraced the faith
of Christ, and entered into the true fold. But this
could not make him forget the Jews, his own brethren
after the flesh, so many of whom were refusing the
salvation which was brought near to them in the
gospel. Not only were they his own people, but
God's own people. God had chosen them out of
other nations to be the honoured messengers of His
truth to mankind. If anything was of God, Israel
was of God. Their want of faith seemed like a
failure of God's purpose.

In this bewilderment light came to St. Paul's
mind, when he took a wider view and considered
the wonderful and unexpected ways in which God's
purposes are carried out at the last. He looked
back on dark times of old, when unbelief had
seemed to prevail, and saw that a true seed of
faithful men had yet lived on and not suffered
the divine light to be wholly quenched. He looked
to those very troubles of the Church in his own time
which were perplexing him, and saw a way of
believing that there too the hand of God was
surely and mightily at work. The rejection of
Christ by the one chosen people was the way to
the admission of all people on earth. The poor,
the maimed, the halt, and the blind were being
gathered in from all the outlying corners of the
world to join in the great feast of the gospel, just

because the chosen guests who had first been invited had refused to come. Thus all things then passing upon earth were indeed through God, even when they seemed to be refusing His guidance.

But lastly, what made this faith really sure and stable was the hope with which St. Paul could look into the future. That unbelief of Israel was but for a time, not for ever. The gifts and callings of God were without repentance; He would never abandon any whom He had chosen for His own. All, Jews and Gentiles alike—God, he says, hath concluded them *all* under sin, that He might have mercy upon *all.* In other words, all things were not only of or from God, not only through God, but also unto God. He could endure all the contradictions and disappointments of the present, because in the dim future at the end of all things he saw the final triumph of God and His everlasting will, holy to the last, loving to the last. Well might he interrupt his epistle with a hymn of praise: "O the depth of the riches and the wisdom and knowledge of God! how unsearchable are his judgments, and his ways past finding out!" Well might he think the only true ending to his confession of faith to be, "To whom be glory for ever. Amen."

These were St. Paul's thoughts. The particular events which called them forth in his mind have long since passed. But the light which came to him was the light of God's counsel and will as they may be seen at all times. He was not staggered at the mournful unbelief of his countrymen, because God's unchanging purpose was present to his mind; and again the light was reflected back, so that his own perplexities of the moment at last enabled him to trust God's unchanging purpose more completely than before. We shall therefore be acting entirely in his spirit, if we apply the text to our own thoughts without dwelling longer on those which weighed on him. There is no great single sorrow and anxiety in our case as there was in his. But we may properly and usefully employ the text to teach us needful truths about our whole lives. Let us take the different parts of the text in their order, for they are all essential.

First "*of* Him," that is, "*from* Him," "are all things." From what or from whom are we? We say that the fruit comes from the flower, the flower from the plant, the plant from the seed. What then do *we* come from? What is the beginning of our life? First of course we come from our parents. It is they who have brought us into being. Without them we should never have lived at all. But from them has come much more than our bare existence; from them or from their parents has come likewise the form of our faces and our bodies; from them too no small part of the form of our minds, what we call our character. Their likeness is carried on in us. We inherit, as we say, from them some of their features without, some of their tempers and dispositions within. All this is meant when we say that we are of or from our parents.

But the Bible teaches us that before and beyond our parents lies God Himself. We are His children, His offspring. The long chain of births and generations which leads back from ourselves to the beginning of the world is all from God. He brought mankind into being, whatever may have been the manner in which our race originated. He gave them the power to bear children like themselves. Nay, we are permitted to believe that we are more nearly related to Him than all the rest of creation. In spite of our sin and our weakness, we have in our nature something God-like; something, that is, of a likeness to God such as we find between a child and its parent.

But again there is much in us that we do not carry with us from our birth. Our bodies could not have lived, much less have grown to their present stature, without food. The earth has given us of its richness to keep us alive, and to enable us to gain the height of manhood. The corn and other produce of the fields, and the cattle which graze upon them, have all helped to make us what we now find ourselves. From them too we are. But can we forget that it is God who causes the seed to swell and burst in the earth, and the plant to grow to its full form, till its fruit is duly ripened? that it is God who gives our bodies the power of turning the food we eat into a support of their own frame, and supplying their own waste from things which to the outward eye are so unlike themselves? Not by bread alone does man live, but by every word that proceeds from the mouth of God. From Him then are we in the support and growth of our bodies.

And then our minds; they too are not left such as they were at birth. Not only do they grow with

s

the body, but they need and they receive supplies of
their own. From our earliest years we are learning;
learning from our parents and teachers, from our
brothers and sisters, from our companions and
friends. From these always, and whether we know
it or not. Thus a great part of our minds, such
as they are now, is from all these different persons,
who have been teaching us in one way or another
all our lives. But again yet more are we *from God*
in this respect as in the others. He is the one
universal, never-ceasing Teacher from the beginning.
All other teachers are but tools in His hand, and He
uses countless other means of teaching us, though we
do not commonly recognize the work which they
perform upon us. Sometimes indeed we say that
this or that man has "received a lesson"; and if we
fully understood and believed our own words, we
should know the truth to be that God has been
teaching him in some marked way. But it is better
and more charitable for us to watch and see how
God teaches ourselves, and in what various ways,
ways of little mark, He is ever carrying on His
lessons within us. If we have learned anything of
wisdom, if we can now walk on our way through life
with fewer stumbles than when we began, to Him it
is all owing. In the growth and nurture of our
hearts and minds as well as of our bodies, *of Him* are
we. With us it has rested whether to receive and
profit by His teaching, or to despise it and waste it.
The truly wise are they who have welcomed it and
made it their own. But the one crowning lesson of
wisdom, the one thought that must fill the mind of

any man who really knows himself, and looks back
over all his past life and sees what he has gained,
and how hardly he has gained it, is summed up in
those familiar words of the psalm, "It is he that
hath made us, and not we ourselves."

Next we read that *through* God are all things.
Here we have to think not so much of ourselves
as of what happens to us. All who grow to full
age have a checkered and varied life. All have
their turn of good and evil. Whence then come
this good and this evil, such good and evil, that
is, as do not come from within? Obviously from
innumerable things which may however be collected
under a few heads. We receive good and evil from
our birth and station in life, from our occupations
when we grow up, from our relations and friends and
neighbours, from the sky and the weather, the air and
the earth, from great changes which fall on men elsewhere in other parts of England, or even other parts
of the world, and at last touch us wherever we are,
changes of politics, of war and peace, of famines and
pestilences, of human passions of all kinds, the desire
of freedom and the lust of conquest, sympathy and
love, jealousy and hatred. All these things, whether
far or near, are the instruments *through which* we are.
They are affecting us at every moment of our lives,
bringing to us changes of fortune, or health, or happiness, or some other of the possessions which make up
the whole of our existence. Yet behind all this com-
plex world which we feel pressing upon us sits God
Himself, ever upholding and guiding, lifting up and
pulling down. Nothing befalls us but by His will.

The purposes of His providence are ruling all the mazy powers, known and unknown, which encompass us on every side. To confess Him as a present God, an ever active and all-knowing providence, is in effect to say that in the truest sense *through Him* are we, and *through Him* are all things.

St. Paul goes on to say, " *Unto him* are all things." Here we stand on different ground. We have some little knowledge of what we are, how we came to be what we are, and how the course of the world is daily maintaining or altering our lot, adding this and taking that away. But all this knowledge, imperfect though it be, fails us completely when we try to look forward and imagine what the world will be by-and-bye, and still more what *we* shall be by-and-bye. Apart from God, we can find hardly any answer to the question, Unto what are we? Unto what are all things? Thus much we know, that the mere dust out of which our bodies are fashioned must sooner or later crumble back to its kindred dust. But when the dust is gone, what and where shall *we* be? Except in the light of God, we could only guess most dimly at an answer. Even now we can only see or speak by pictures and images: the realities of the unseen world remain behind the veil. But we can be content to let it be so, if we hold fast St. Paul's faith without wavering. " Unto God are all things." He is the end, the goal towards which all things move in heaven and earth, the one great sea into which all the wandering rivers run. The words we use must be dim, for the thought itself is dim, but it

contains within it a glorious hope, a hope full of
awful warning, but still a hope which cannot be
quenched except by forgetting the character of
God, or failing to trust Him to the uttermost.
Such as we have found Him here, such we shall
find Him in the hidden future. His hatred of sin
cannot cease, for sin is what makes us unlike Him,
and His never-ending work upon us is to mould us
after His own likeness. His love of every creature
whom He has made cannot cease, for that is the
deepest thing that we can know of His nature.
In what way His purposes shall be wrought out,
we cannot tell. It is enough for us to know what
He is, and to know that He cannot change.

Let us now look back and consider what we
have been learning on this the last Sunday of the
Christian year. Beyond all the beginnings *from*
which we and all things came, we have found God
and found all things taking their birth *from Him*.
Beyond all the powers of the world *through which*
our life is bent hither and thither we have found
God, and found all things guided by His will, coming
to pass, that is, *through Him*. And then, gazing
into the darkness before us, we have learned from
St. Paul, gathering up as he did the teaching of
the whole Bible explained and brought to a head
in the gospel, to see by faith God still before us
in that most wonderful "beyond," to see ourselves
and all things moving ever nearer and nearer *to
Him*, and to trust ourselves to the purposes of His
love as they are revealed in His Blessed Son. Can
we then go on living as if all this meant nothing?

Is it nothing to know that whichever way we turn, behind, or around or before, we are met at every point by the power and presence of our everlasting Lord? Can we think that we do well to choose our daily path only by the little thoughts and wishes of our little life, and to give no heed to the laws of that kingdom of the Most High which closes us in on every side as the sky closes in the earth? The earth has terrible power to draw our eyes ever downward. But why are we so slow to resist its enticements? Why do we not oftener lift up our eyes to the heaven above, and remember that we are children of a heavenly King?

GLASGOW: PRINTED AT THE UNIVERSITY PRESS BY ROBERT MACLEHOSE AND CO.

For EU product safety concerns, contact us at Calle de José Abascal, 56–1°,
28003 Madrid, Spain or eugpsr@cambridge.org.

www.ingramcontent.com/pod-product-compliance
Ingram Content Group UK Ltd.
Pitfield, Milton Keynes, MK11 3LW, UK
UKHW010347140625
459647UK00010B/890